MORE CREATIVE
window
treatments

Complete step-by-step instructions with full-color photos
for over 60 distinctive window treatments

CREATIVE
PUBLISHING
international

MINNETONKA, MINNESOTA

President/CEO: Michael Eleftheriou

Executive Editor: Elaine Perry
Senior Editor: Linda Neubauer
Project Manager: Linnéa Christensen
Senior Art Director: Stephanie Michaud
Desktop Publishing Specialist: Laurie Kristensen
Editorial Intern: Andrew Karre
Technical Photo Stylists: Bridget Haugh, Susan Jorgensen,
  Nancy Sundeen
Project Stylist: Joanne Wawra
Prop Stylist: Michele Joy
Sewing Staff: Arlene Dohrman, Sharon Ecklund,
  Phyllis Galbraith, Valerie Hill, Kristi Kuhnau,
  Virginia Mateen, Ginger Mountin, Carol Pilot,
  Michelle Skudlarek, Nancy Sundeen
Studio Services Manager: Marcia Chambers
Lead Photographer: Charles Nields
Photographers: Rebecca Hawthorne, Kevin Hedden,
  Rex Irmen, Billy Lindner, Mark Macemon, Mike Parker,
  Greg Wallace
Contributing Photographers: Phil Aarrestad, Kim Bailey,
  Doug Cummelin, Doug Deutscher, Paul England,
  Mark Hardy, Chris Kausch, Steve Smith
Print Production Manager: Mary Ann Knox
Scenic Carpenters: Jon Hegge, Troy Johnson,
  Rob Johnstone, John Nadeau
Consultants: Julie Anderson, Jo Ann Brezette,
  Kathy Ellingson, Steve Engler, Amy Engman,
  Wendy Fedie, Patrick Kartes, Janis Kieft
Contributors: American and Efird, Inc./Mettler; Conso
  Products Company; Dritz Corporation; General Clutch;

Graber Industries, Inc./Springs Window Fashion
Division; Handler Textile Corporation; Kirsch Division,
Cooper Industries, Inc.; Krifon; Joyce Oakle; The Singer
Company; Springs Industries; Swavelle/Mill Creek
Textiles; Waverly, Division of F. Schumacher &
Company

MORE CREATIVE WINDOW TREATMENTS
Created by: The Editors of
  Creative Publishing international, Inc.

Printed on American paper by:
R. R. Donnelley & Sons Co.
10 9 8 7 6 5 4 3

Creative Publishing international, Inc. offers a variety of
how-to books. For information write:
  Creative Publishing international, Inc.
    Subscriber Books
  5900 Green Oak Drive
  Minnetonka, MN 55343

contents

WINDOW TREATMENT STYLES

With careful style selection,
window treatments can be
both functional and beautiful.

Window treatments have a great impact on the decorating scheme of a room. Depending on the style of the treatment and the fabric selected, a window can become a dramatic focal point in the room. Or it can blend with the wall treatment, creating a subtle background and allowing the furniture to take center stage. Style choices vary from simple, informal treatments, such as fabric roller shades or scarf swags, to boldly formal layered curtains and elaborate top treatments.

Along with the decorative aspects of the window treatment, there are a few functional needs to consider. Bedroom windows, for instance, may require a high degree of light control, while window treatments in the dining room may be selected because they allow light to fill the room. Treatments that offer privacy may be necessary on windows that face a busy street, while windows that open onto a beautiful, secluded landscape may be dressed with minimal treatments that merely enhance the view.

Whether you are starting with bare windows or adding to existing treatments, such as pleated shades or blinds, you can select a window treatment that reflects your personal taste. Careful selection of style, fabric, and hardware helps ensure the success of your window treatment project.

SELECTING A STYLE

Aside from the decorative and functional aspects of the window treatment, also consider the structural details of the window itself, including the way it operates. The treatment must be designed to allow easy access if the window will be opened and closed regularly. You may want to accent a decorative window frame or select a style that will cover inferior woodwork around the window. Also take note of any structural details near the window that may affect the size or style of the treatment, such as built-in cabinets, electrical switches, doors, heat registers, or other windows.

Often the window treatment you select will be a combination of two or more styles. One style, selected for its functional characteristics, may be combined with another decorative style to satisfy all the needs of the treatment. For consistency, combine styles that reflect the same decorating theme. Some choices, such as fabric roller shades and scarf swags, are versatile and can be combined successfully with many other styles.

Snapshots of windows *serve as visual aides when selecting window treatments. Take a photograph of the window, closing any existing undertreatments that will remain; catch the ceiling line and floor in the photograph. Cover the photograph with a sheet of clear plastic or acetate, and, using a dry-erase marker, sketch the desired treatment.*

Rod-pocket curtains with welted heading *(page 45) are tied back with shaped tiebacks (page 54). Scarf swag valance (page 78) is mounted over the top of the curtains, allowing the heading to show.*

Ruffled rod-pocket swag *(page 73) is an elegant complement to these sheer rod-pocket curtains (page 42).*

Soft cornice with overlapping panels (page 100) softens the contemporary look of vertical blinds.

Stagecoach valance (page 84) is mounted inside the window frame.

Straw hats hung from a peg rail (page 124) make an interesting alternative-style valance.

Unlined rod-pocket curtains have a flounce heading (page 44) and shaped tiebacks (page 54). African violets add a touch of color to the treatment (page 109).

Hourglass curtains (page 61) are the perfect treatment for French doors.

(Continued)

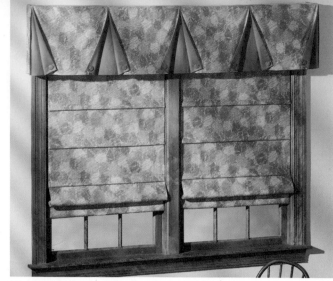

Slatted Roman shades (page 30) have a sleek, contemporary look, which is also carried out by the buttoned valance (page 90).

Split hourglass curtains (page 66) frame a frosted design (page 111) on a door window.

Hanging plant shelf (page 104) is a functional alternative window treatment.

Rod-pocket curtains with double ruffles (page 50) are layered over a fabric roller shade (page 34). Ruffled tiebacks (page 55) complete the look.

Scarf swags with poufs (page 78) are an elegant top treatment over pleated shades.

Shoji-style screen (page 114) is a simplified version of the traditional Japanese window treatment.

Hobbled Roman shade (page 25), mounted outside the window frame, is an understated treatment for a small window.

Lined rod-pocket curtains (page 43) mounted on a PVC pole with elbows (page 14) are held back gracefully with decorative holdbacks (page 10).

Hourglass curtains (page 61) and split hourglass curtains (page 66) are combined to make a unique treatment for this triple window.

Triple rod-pocket swag (page 76) with tassel fringe trim is a soft yet dramatic top treatment over sheer curtains.

Whether your window treatment is stationary or traversing, the hardware you select can be decorative as well as functional. For ornate window treatments, traditional wood or metal poles with detailed finials are available, as well as decorative tieback holders. And sleek, contemporary hardware is available for a more understated look. Some treatment styles cover the rod entirely, calling for less expensive, nondecorative utility hardware.

Select and install the hardware you want before measuring for a window treatment. The cut length of fabric panels for curtains, draperies, and valances depends on the style and placement of the hardware.

DECORATIVE HARDWARE

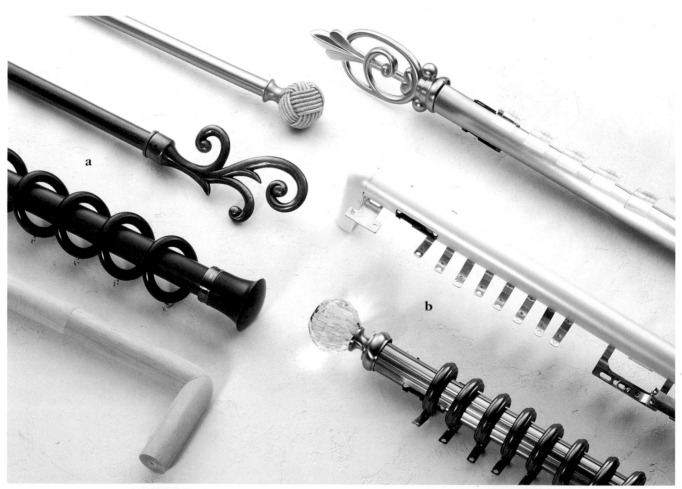

Metal rods and wood poles (a) in various finishes and diameters are used with rings for hand-drawn traversing or stationary treatments when part or all of the rod or pole is always exposed. Without the rings, the rods and poles are suitable for swags or for stationary rod-pocket or tab styles. Stylish finials accompany the metal rods; wood poles may have finials or elbows. Unfinished wood poles can be painted, stained, or covered with fabric to fit perfectly into your decor.

Decorative traverse rods (b) have a built-in mechanism of carriers and cording for opening and closing the treatment. Most often used for pleated draperies, the rods can have plain carriers or ring carriers. Tab carriers are also available, for hanging traversing tab curtains.

UTILITY HARDWARE

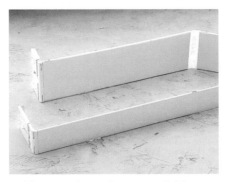

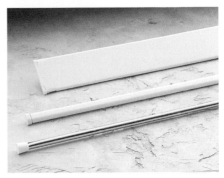

Narrow curtain rods are used for rod-pocket window treatments. They are available in various projections in single and double rod styles.

Wide curtain rods are available in 2½" (6.5 cm) and 4½" (11.5 cm) widths. They add depth and interest to rod pocket window treatments. Corner connectors make these rods suitable for bay and corner windows, also.

Tension rods, used inside window frames for rod pocket curtains and valances, are held in place by the pressure of a spring inside the rod. Because mounting brackets are not used, the woodwork is not damaged by screws.

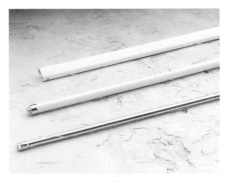

Sash rods use shallow mounting brackets so the window treatment hangs close to the glass. Available flat or round, they are commonly used for stretched curtains on doors.

Conventional traverse rods, designed for pleated draperies, are available in white, ivory, and wood tones. Drapery hooks are inserted so the pleats conceal the rod when the treatment is closed. Valances or cornices are used over the top of the draperies to completely conceal the rod.

Flexible traverse rods are used for pleated draperies on bow windows.

HARDWARE ACCESSORIES

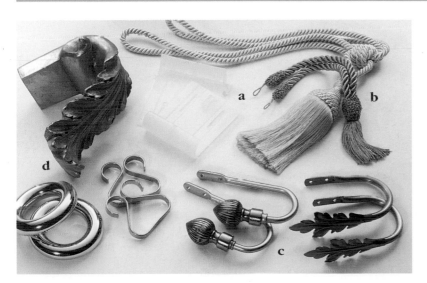

Concealed tieback holders (a) fit behind the last fold of pleated or rod-pocket draperies to prevent the tieback from crushing the draperies. The projection is adjustable.

Cord-and-tassel tiebacks (b) are used with concealed or decorative holders to hold draperies in place.

Holdbacks (c), as the name implies, are decorative accessories that hold back a stationary curtain or drapery without the use of tiebacks.

Swag holders (d), in a wide range of styles, support the draped fabric in swag window treatments. Some styles are meant to be concealed, while others are quite obviously decorative.

INSTALLING HARDWARE

Window treatment hardware is packaged complete with mounting brackets, screws or nails, and installation instructions. Use screws alone if installing through drywall or plaster directly into wall studs. When brackets are positioned between wall studs, support the screws for lightweight treatments with plastic anchors in the correct size for the screws. If the brackets must support a heavy window treatment, use plastic toggle anchors in the correct size for the wallboard depth, or use molly bolts. If nails are supplied with the hardware you purchased, use them only for lightweight treatments installed directly to the window frame. Otherwise, substitute screws or molly bolts that fit through the holes in the brackets.

HOW TO INSTALL HARDWARE USING PLASTIC ANCHORS

1 Mark the screw locations on the wall. Drill holes for the plastic anchors, using a drill bit slightly smaller than the diameter of the plastic anchor. Tap the plastic anchors into the drilled holes, using a hammer.

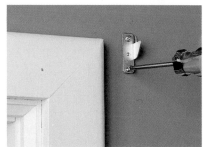

2 Insert the screw through the hole in the hardware and into installed plastic anchor. Tighten the screw securely; the anchor expands in drywall, preventing it from pulling out of the wall.

HOW TO INSTALL HARDWARE USING PLASTIC TOGGLE ANCHORS

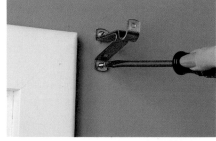

1 Mark screw locations on wall. Drill holes for plastic toggle anchors, using drill bit slightly smaller than diameter of toggle anchor shank.

2 Squeeze the wings of the toggle anchor flat, and push toggle anchor into hole; tap in with hammer until it is flush with wall.

3 Insert the screw through hole in hardware and into installed anchor; tighten screw. Wings spread out and flatten against back side of drywall.

HOW TO INSTALL HARDWARE USING MOLLY BOLTS

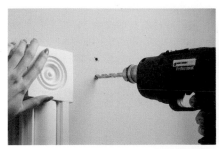

1 Mark screw locations on wall. Drill holes for molly bolts, using drill bit slightly smaller than diameter of the molly bolt.

2 Tap the molly bolt into the drilled hole, using hammer; tighten screw. Molly bolt expands and flattens against back side of drywall.

3 Remove screw from molly bolt; insert the screw through hole in hardware and into installed molly bolt. Screw hardware securely in place.

INSTALLING PVC POLES

Pvc pipe can be used as a lightweight and inexpensive alternative to wood or metal decorator poles. PVC pipe is available in a variety of sizes, with inside diameters ranging from 1" to 4" (2.5 to 10 cm). PVC elbows, available in each size, can be used to make a pole with returns. Or, if desired, decorator finials can be attached to the ends of the PVC pole.

MATERIALS

FOR POLES WITH FINIALS

- PVC pipe in desired diameter; select size of pipe to fit end of finial.
- Two decorator finials.
- Keyhole support brackets, for ends and center supports; ½" (1.3 cm) hex-head screws.
- 1½" (3.8 cm) hex-head screws, for installing brackets into wall studs; or molly bolts or toggle anchors, for installing into drywall or plaster.
- Scrap of wood.
- Sandpaper; hacksaw; drill and drill bits.

FOR POLES WITH ELBOW RETURNS

- PVC pipe in desired diameter.
- Two PVC elbows, preferably without collars, in size to match pipe.
- Keyhole support brackets, for center supports; ½" (1.3 cm) hex-head screws.
- Two 2" (5 cm) angle irons, for mounting at returns.
- 1½" (3.8 cm) flat-head screws, for installing angle irons into wall studs; or molly bolts or toggle anchors, for installing into drywall or plaster.
- Two 10 × 1" (2.5 cm) round-head bolts.

HOW TO MAKE & INSTALL A PVC POLE WITH FINIALS

1 Cut PVC pipe to the desired length, using a hacksaw; sand the ends. Cut a scrap of wood to wedge snugly into each end of the pipe. Drill a hole in center of each wood scrap, using a drill bit slightly smaller than the finial screw. Insert the wood scraps into ends of the pole.

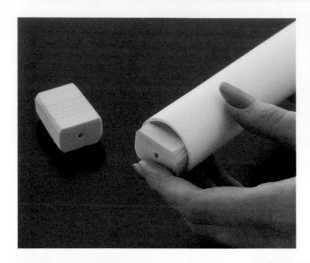

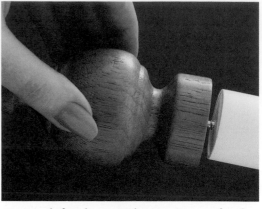

2 Attach finial to wood scrap. Repeat for the opposite end of the pole.

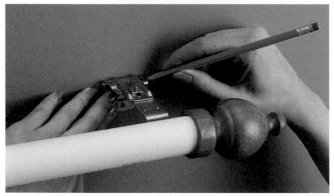

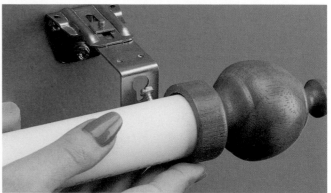

3 Hold the pole to the wall at desired location; mark for placement of keyhole support brackets on wall, at least ½" (1.3 cm) from finials. If additional support bracket is needed, mark for placement near center. Install brackets, using 1½" (3.8 cm) hex-head screws, into wall studs; if brackets are not positioned at the wall studs, use molly bolts or toggle anchors (page 12).

4 Hold pole up to the brackets; mark placement for ½" (1.3 cm) screws on back of the pole. Predrill holes for screws; insert screws into the holes, leaving heads of screws standing slightly away from back of the pole. Mount pole, inserting the screw heads into the keyholes.

HOW TO MAKE & INSTALL A PVC POLE WITH ELBOW RETURNS

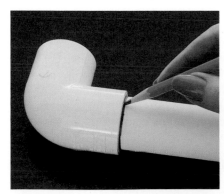

1 Slide elbow onto the pipe as far as possible; mark the depth of elbow on the pipe.

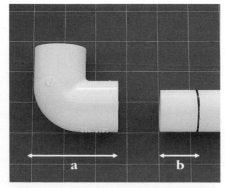

2 Remove elbow; measure the elbow length **(a)** from the outer edge of one side to the opening on the opposite side. Then measure the elbow depth **(b)** from end of pipe to the mark.

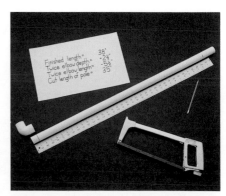

3 Cut the PVC pipe, using hacksaw, with length equal to the desired finished length of the pole plus twice the elbow depth minus twice the elbow length. Sand the cut ends.

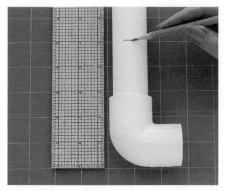

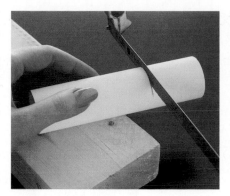

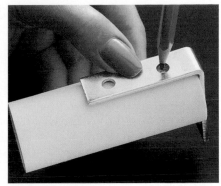

4 Slide the elbow onto a small remaining piece of PVC pipe as far as possible. Measure from the outer edge of elbow to the desired return depth on pipe; mark.

5 Remove the pipe from the elbow. Cut the pipe with a hacksaw; cut a second piece the same length for the opposite return. Sand the cut ends.

6 Lay angle iron over end of return pipe; mark pipe with location of hole closest to the back of angle iron. Drill hole through marked side of the pipe, using a ¼" drill bit. Repeat for the second return pipe.

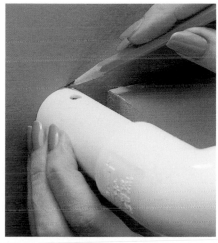

7 Assemble PVC pole, sliding pipe pieces into the elbows as far as possible, with holes in return pieces centered on top. Hold pole to wall in the desired location; mark wall at top center of return piece.

8 Mount angle irons on wall, with tops of angle irons centered at the marks, using 1½" (3.8 cm) flat-head screws into wall studs; if angle irons are not positioned at wall studs, use molly bolts or toggle anchors (page 12). Mount pole over angle irons, aligning holes in pipe to holes in angle irons; insert 10 × 1" (2.5 cm) round-head bolts through holes to secure.

9 Mark the wall for center keyhole support bracket, if needed; mark placement for screw on back of pole. Remove pole; install bracket on wall, and insert screw into back of pole, as in step 4, opposite. Remount pole.

HOW TO HANG ROD-POCKET CURTAINS ON A PVC POLE

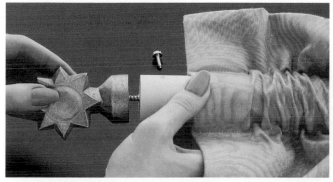

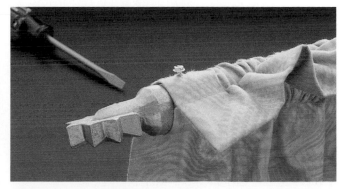

1 Remove pole from wall; remove screws, if any, from the back of pole. Remove elbows or finials. Insert the pole into rod pocket of the curtain; reattach finials or elbows. Distribute fullness evenly.

2 Locate screw holes, if any, and insert screws through curtain fabric. Remount the pole on the brackets or angle irons.

INSTALLING MOUNTING BOARDS

Many window treatments are mounted on boards rather than on drapery hardware. The mounting board is covered with fabric to match the window treatment or with drapery lining, and the window treatment is then stapled to the board. The mounting board can be installed as an outside mount, securing it directly to the window frame or to the wall above and outside the window frame. Or the board may be installed as an inside mount by securing it inside the window frame.

The size of the mounting board varies, depending on whether the board-mounted window treatment is an inside or outside mount and whether it is being used alone or with an undertreatment. When using stock, or nominal, lumber, keep in mind that the actual measurement differs from the nominal measurement. A 1 × 2 board measures 3/4" × 1 1/2" (2 × 3.8 cm), a 1 × 4 measures 3/4" × 3 1/2" (2 × 9 cm), a 1 × 6 measures 3/4" × 5 1/2" (2 × 14 cm), and a 1 × 8 measures 3/4" × 7 1/4" (2 × 18.7 cm).

For an inside-mounted window treatment, the depth of the window frame must be at least 1 1/2" (3.8 cm), to accommodate a 1 × 2 mounting board. Cut the mounting board 1/2" (1.3 cm) shorter than the inside measurement across the window frame, to ensure that the board will fit inside the frame after it is covered with fabric.

The projection necessary for outside-mounted top treatments depends on the projection of any existing undertreatments. If the undertreatment is stationary, allow at least 2" (5 cm) of clearance between it and the top treatment; if the undertreatment traverses, allow at least 3" (7.5 cm) clearance. If there is no undertreatment or if the undertreatment is mounted inside the window frame, use a 1 × 4 board for the top treatment. Cut the mounting board at least 2" (5 cm) wider than the outside measurement across the window frame. Install the board using angle irons that measure more than one-half the projection of the board.

For an outside-mounted Roman shade, use a 1 × 2 board. Screw the board flat to the wall for a 3/4" (2 cm) projection; this allows the shade to rest close to the window frame. For a 1 1/2" (3.8 cm) projection, install the board on edge, using angle irons.

HOW TO COVER THE MOUNTING BOARD

CUTTING DIRECTIONS

Cut the fabric to cover the mounting board, with the width of the fabric equal to the distance around the mounting board plus 1" (2.5 cm) and the length of the fabric equal to the length of the mounting board plus 3" (7.5 cm).

1 Center board on the wrong side of the fabric. Staple one long edge of fabric to board, placing staples about 8" (20.5 cm) apart; do not staple within 6" (15 cm) of ends. Wrap the fabric around board. Fold under 3/8" (1 cm) on long edge; staple to board, placing staples about 6" (15 cm) apart.

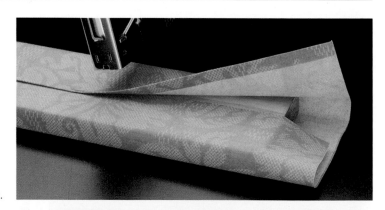

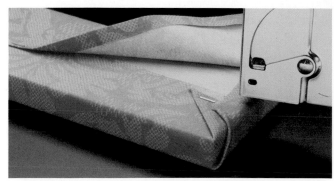

2 Miter fabric at corners on side of board with unfolded fabric edge; finger-press. Staple miters in place near raw edge.

3 Miter fabric at corners on side of board with folded fabric edge; finger-press. Fold under excess fabric at ends; staple near fold.

HOW TO INSTALL AN INSIDE-MOUNTED BOARD

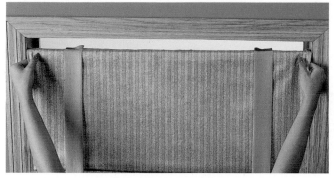

1 Cover mounting board (opposite). Attach the window treatment to the mounting board. Hold board in place against upper window frame, with wide side of board up; align front of treatment with front edge of frame.

2 Predrill screw holes through the board and up into the window frame, using ⅛" drill bit; drill holes within 1" (2.5 cm) of each end of the board and in center for wide window treatments. Adjust placement of holes to avoid screw eyes, if any. Secure the board, using 8 × 1½" (3.8 cm) round-head screws.

HOW TO INSTALL AN OUTSIDE-MOUNTED BOARD

1 Cover mounting board (opposite). Attach window treatment to board. Mark screw holes for angle irons on bottom of board, positioning angle irons within 1" (2.5 cm) of each end of board and at 45" (115 cm) intervals or less; adjust the placement to avoid screw eyes, if any.

2 Predrill screw holes into board; size of drill bit depends on screw size required for angle iron. Screw angle irons to board.

3 Hold board at desired placement, making sure it is level; mark the screw holes on wall or window frame. Remove angle irons from board.

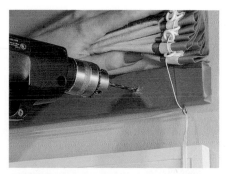

4 Secure angle irons to wall, using 1½" (3.8 cm) flat-head screws, into wall studs; if angle irons are not positioned at wall studs, use molly bolts or toggle anchors instead of flat-head screws.

5 Reposition window treatment on angle irons, aligning screw holes; fasten screws.

Roman shade mounted with ¾" (2 cm) projection. Install board flat to wall at desired location above window, predrilling holes through board into wall. Secure with 8 × 2½" (6.5 cm) flat-head screws into wall studs, if possible; or use molly bolts or toggle anchors if not screwing into wall studs.

MEASURING

Sketch the window treatment to scale on graph paper, to help you determine the most pleasing proportion for the treatment as well as the correct placement of any necessary hardware. After installing the hardware, take all necessary measurements of the window, using a steel tape measure for accuracy, and record the measurements on the sketch.

Window treatments may be mounted inside or outside the window frame, depending on the style of the treatment and the depth of the frame. For an inside mount, the frame must be deep enough to allow the treatment to be mounted flush with the front of the frame and without interfering with the operation of the window. For an outside mount, the hardware may be mounted on the window frame or on the wall outside the frame, high enough to allow any center support brackets to clear the frame.

For each project, you will need to determine the finished length and width of the treatment. The finished length is measured from the top of the mounting board, rod, or heading to where you want the lower edge of the window treatment. The finished width is determined by measuring the length of the rod or mounting board; for treatments with returns, add twice the projection of the rod or mounting board.

Specific instructions for determining the cut lengths and widths of the fabric are given for each project in this book. Yardage requirements can be determined by multiplying the cut length by the number of fabric widths needed to obtain the cut width. When estimating the yardage for patterned fabric, add the length of one pattern repeat for each fabric width needed, to allow for matching the patterns.

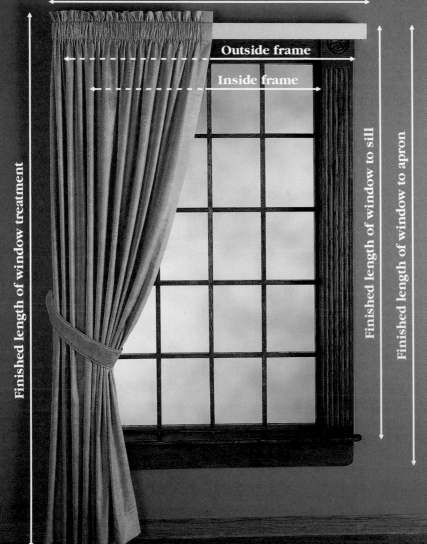

Finished width of window treatment or length of rod or mounting board plus returns

Outside frame

Inside frame

Finished length of window treatment

Finished length of window to sill

Finished length of window to apron

TIPS FOR MEASURING

Plan the proportion of the layers in a window treatment so the length of the top treatment is about one-fifth the length of the undertreatment. The top treatment may be installed higher than the window, to add visual height to the overall treatment. In some cases, it may be desirable to start the top treatment at the ceiling, provided the top of the window frame is not visible at the lower edge of the top treatment.

Plan for the shortest point of a top treatment to fall at least 4" to 6" (10 to 15 cm) below the top of the window glass. This prevents you from seeing the window frame as you look upward at the top treatment.

Allow ½" (1.3 cm) clearance between the lower edge of the curtain panels and the floor when measuring for floor-length curtains. Allow 1" (2.5 cm) clearance for loosely woven fabrics, because the curtains may stretch slightly after they are hung.

Allow 4" to 6" (10 to 15 cm) clearance above baseboard heaters, for safety.

Plan window treatments to avoid covering heat registers or cold-air returns, for good air circulation.

Measure for all curtains in the room to the same height from the floor, for a uniform look. Use the highest window in the room as the standard for measuring the other windows.

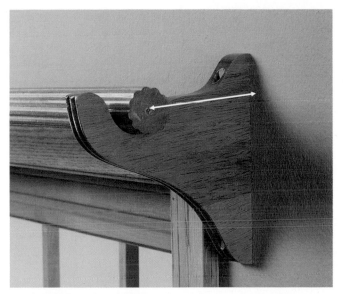

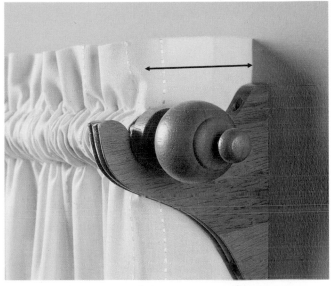

Projection is the distance the rod or mounting board stands out from the wall. When a wood pole is used, the projection is the distance from the wall to the center of the pole.

Return is the portion of the curtain or top treatment extending from the end of the rod or mounting board to the wall, enclosing the brackets and blocking the side light and view.

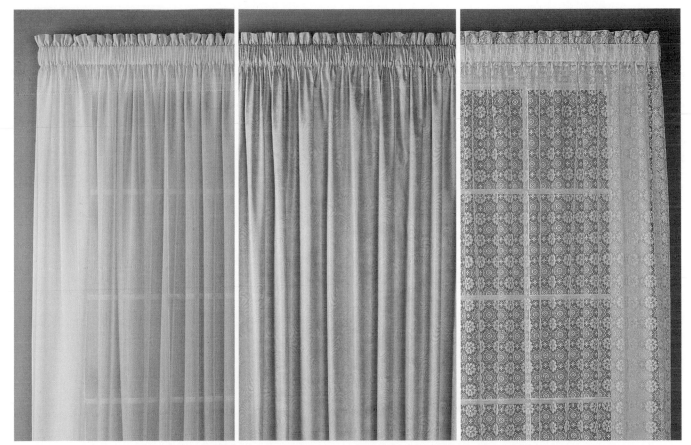

Fullness describes the finished width of the curtain panels in proportion to the length of the rod. For example, two times fullness means that the width of the curtain measures two times the length of the rod. For sheer and lightweight fabrics, use two-and-one-half to three times fullness (left). For mediumweight to heavyweight fabrics, use two to two-and-one-half times fullness (center). For lace curtains, one-and-one-half to two times fullness is often used, allowing the pattern in the lace to be more apparent (right).

BASIC SEWING TECHNIQUES

When sewing window treatments, a few basic guidelines help ensure good results. The techniques vary somewhat, depending on the type of fabric you are sewing. For any project, it is important to preshrink fabric and lining, using a steam iron, before they are cut.

Many decorator fabrics are tightly woven and may be cut perpendicular to the selvage, using a carpenter's square as a guide for marking the cutting line. However, because lightweight and loosely woven fabrics, such as sheers and casements, tend to slide easily as you cut, it is easier and more accurate to pull a thread along the crosswise grain and cut along the pulled thread.

Patterned decorator fabrics are designed to be matched at the seams (opposite). For soft cornices, stagecoach valances, and other window treatments with wide, flat expanses of fabric, it is desirable to eliminate seams by railroading the fabric whenever possible (opposite).

Many window treatments look better and are more durable if they are lined. Lining adds body to the treatment as well as protection from sunlight. Some linings are treated to be water-resistant, while others provide a higher degree of energy efficiency or light control. Blackout lining (opposite) not only blocks the sunlight, but also helps to conceal seams and hems.

TYPES OF SEAMS

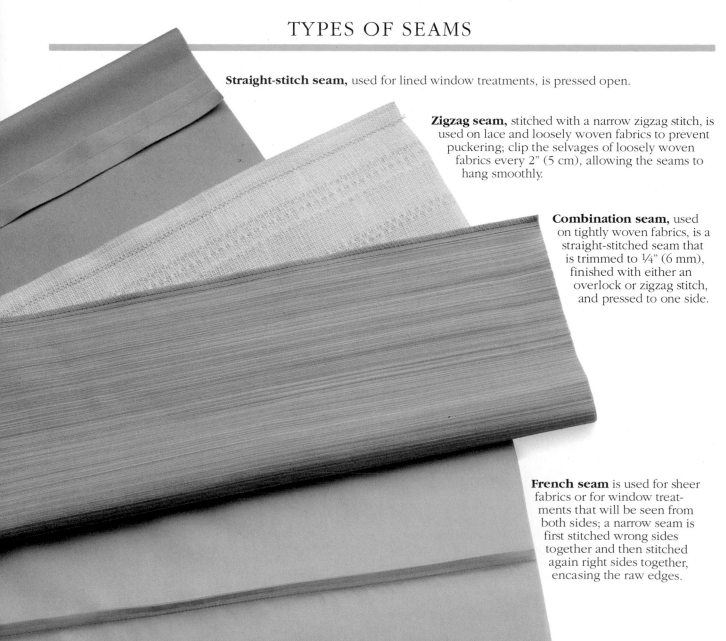

Straight-stitch seam, used for lined window treatments, is pressed open.

Zigzag seam, stitched with a narrow zigzag stitch, is used on lace and loosely woven fabrics to prevent puckering; clip the selvages of loosely woven fabrics every 2" (5 cm), allowing the seams to hang smoothly.

Combination seam, used on tightly woven fabrics, is a straight-stitched seam that is trimmed to ¼" (6 mm), finished with either an overlock or zigzag stitch, and pressed to one side.

French seam is used for sheer fabrics or for window treatments that will be seen from both sides; a narrow seam is first stitched wrong sides together and then stitched again right sides together, encasing the raw edges.

MATCHING PATTERNED FABRICS

1 Position fabric widths right sides together, matching selvages. Fold back upper selvage until the pattern matches; press foldline.

2 Unfold selvage, and pin the fabric widths together on foldline. Check the match from right side.

3 Repin the fabric so the pins are perpendicular to foldline; stitch on the foldline, using straight stitch.

CONSTRUCTION TIPS

Railroad fabric by running the lengthwise grain horizontally on window treatments with wide, flat expanses, as shown in the soft cornice at left. If fabric is not railroaded, as shown in the example at right, it is necessary to seam the fabric. Railroading is appropriate for fabrics with solid colors or nondirectional patterns.

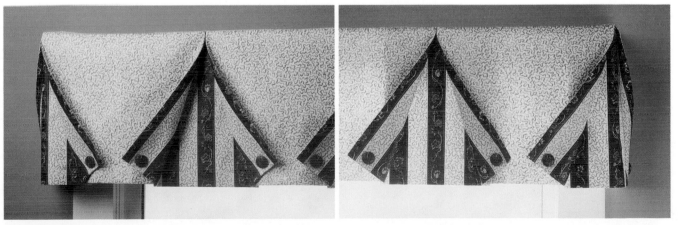

Blackout lining, used for the valance at left, blocks light completely. This prevents unsightly shadowing of seams, hems, or designs from the back of the treatment onto the front, as shown in the example at right.

Window Shades

HOBBLED ROMAN SHADES

Hobbled Roman shades are constructed with soft horizontal folds that add interest and dimension. Rings are stitched to the wrong side of the shade through vertical rows of twill tape. Because the shade is visually interrupted by the folds, best results are achieved with plain fabrics or all over prints.

The shade is attached to a mounting board and can be installed as either an inside or outside mount (pages 16 and 17). A weight bar inserted into the lower hem helps the shade hang smoothly.

CALCULATING THE RING SPACING

The distance between rings can vary, depending on the desired look for the shade. A distance of 4" (10 cm) between rings is attractive for most windows; because the length of fabric in each fold is equal to twice the distance between the rings, this requires 8" (20.5 cm) of fabric for each fold. It is helpful to diagram the shade as shown below, drawing in the spaces between the rings and the number of folds.

For an outside-mounted shade, if the estimated finished length of the shade is not evenly divisible by the desired space between the rings, the measurement for the finished length can be rounded up until it is, provided there is the necessary wall space above the window for mounting. For example, if you would like 4" (10 cm) spaces between the rings and the estimated finished length is 45" (115 cm), you can round up the measurement to a 48" (122 cm) finished length, which is divisible by four. This allows for a 4" (10 cm) hem depth, ten 4" (10 cm) spaces between the rings, and 4" (10 cm) between the top ring and the top of the mounting board.

If the length of the shade cannot be adjusted, as is the case with an inside-mounted shade that must fit within the window frame, the spacing between the rings can be adjusted. For example, a shade measuring 45" (115 cm) in length can be constructed with a 4½" (11.5 cm) hem depth and nine 4½" (11.5 cm) spaces, including the space between the top ring and the top of the mounting board. Another alternative is a 5" (12.5 cm) hem depth and eight 5" (12.5 cm) spaces.

MAKING A DIAGRAM OF THE SHADE

1 Diagram side view of the hobbled shade, including the hem, the correct number of spaces between rings, and length of fabric in the folds. Label the finished length of the shade, the distance between rings, and the hem depth. The hem depth and the distance between top ring and top of board are equal to the distance between rings.

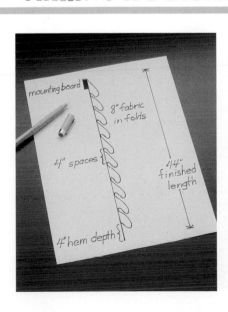

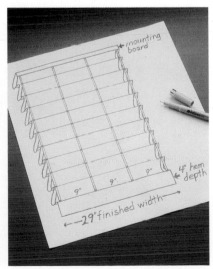

2 Diagram the shade from the back, indicating the number of vertical rows of twill tape and rings, and the spacing between the rows. Place one row 1" (2.5 cm) from each side, and evenly space remaining rows 8" to 12" (20.5 to 30.5 cm) apart across the shade.

MATERIALS

- Decorator fabric.
- Lining fabric.
- Fusible web, ½" (1.3 cm) wide.
- ½" (1.3 cm) plastic rings.
- ½" (1.3 cm) polyester twill tape; to determine yardage needed, multiply number of rows by finished shade length.
- 1 × 2 mounting board, cut to length as determined on page 16.

- Screw eyes, one for each row of twill tape and rings.
- Shade cord.
- Awning cleat.
- Weight bar, ¼" (6 mm) to ⅜" (1 cm) in diameter; wood dowel, aluminum rod, or brass rod may be used.
- 1½" (3.8 cm) angle irons with flat-head screws, for installing an outside-mounted shade.

- 8 × 2½" (6.5 cm) flat-head screws, for installing outside-mounted valance into wall studs; or molly bolts or toggle anchors, for installing outside-mounted shade into drywall or plaster.
- 8 × 1½" (3.8 cm) round-head screws, for installing an inside-mounted shade.
- Staple gun and staples.
- Drill and ⅛" drill bit.

CUTTING DIRECTIONS

Determine the finished length of the shade from the top of the mounting board to either the sill or ½" (1.3 cm) below the bottom of the apron.

Determine the finished width of the shade. For an outside mount, the shade should extend at least 1" (2.5 cm) beyond the window frame on each side. For an inside mount, measure the inside of the window frame from side to side at the top, middle, and bottom; subtract ⅛" (3 mm) from the narrowest of these measurements for the finished width of the shade.

The cut length of the shade fabric is equal to twice the finished length of the shade plus the hem depth plus the projection of the mounting board (page 16). The cut width of the shade fabric is equal to the finished width of the

shade plus 3" (7.5 cm). If more than one width of fabric is needed for the shade, use a complete width for the center of the shade and seam equal partial widths to each side.

Cut the lining to the cut length of the shade fabric minus twice the hem depth. The cut width of the lining is equal to the finished width of the shade.

Determine the number of rows of twill tape needed; steam-press the tape to preshrink it, and cut each piece to the length of the finished shade.

Cut the weight bar ½" (1.3 cm) shorter than the finished width of the shade.

Cut the fabric to cover the mounting board.

HOW TO MAKE A HOBBLED ROMAN SHADE

1 Seam fabric widths together, if necessary; trim to the cut width determined above. Repeat for lining fabric. Stabilize the side edges by applying liquid fray preventer or by finishing the edges, using overlock or zigzag stitch. Press under 1½" (3.8 cm) on each side, for the hems.

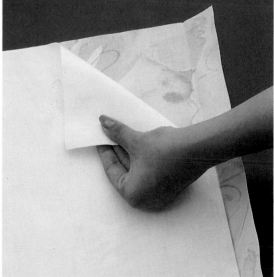

2 Place shade fabric facedown on flat surface. Place lining on the shade fabric, wrong sides together, with upper edges matching. Place lining under the side hems, up to foldlines.

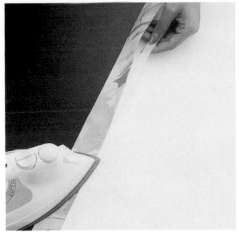

3 Fuse the side hems over the lining, using ½" (1.3 cm) strips of fusible web.

4 Press under an amount equal to the hem depth at lower edge of shade fabric; then press under again, to make double-fold hem. Pin in place.

5 Mark a line across top of shade to indicate projection of mounting board. Mark placement for rings in first vertical row, 1" (2.5 cm) from side of shade, with top mark 8" (20.5 cm) below marked line for projection and with bottom mark at upper edge of hem. Space marks a distance apart equal to twice the distance between rings as calculated on page 25; repeat for opposite side.

6 Mark placement for rings in the first horizontal row at upper edge of hem, spacing rows as determined in your diagram of shade (page 25). Continue marking placement for all remaining rings. Pin the lining to shade fabric at each ring placement mark.

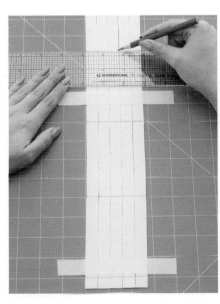

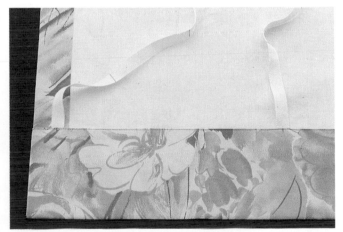

7 Tape or pin lengths of twill tape, side by side, to work surface. Mark a line across tapes, ½" (1.3 cm) from one end. Mark additional lines across the tapes, spacing marks as calculated for distance between the rings.

8 Insert ½" (1.3 cm) ends of tapes under top edge of hem up to first line, centering one tape at each ring placement mark; pin in place. Stitch hem in place, catching tapes in stitching.

(Continued)

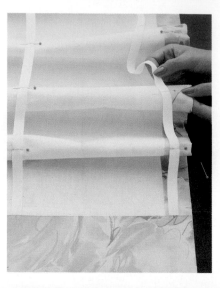

9 Pin the twill tapes to ring marks, beginning at the bottom of the shade, centering the tapes on the ring marks and pinning through all the layers.

10 Attaching rings by machine. Set zigzag stitch at the widest setting; set stitch length at 0. Fold shade, right sides together, along first horizontal row of pins. Place ring next to folded edge. At center of twill tape, stitch over the ring and folded edge with about eight stitches. Secure the stitches by stitching in place for two or three stitches, with the stitch width and length set at 0. Repeat for remaining horizontal rows.

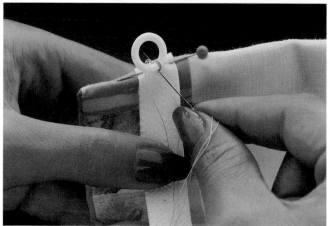

10 Attaching rings by hand. Tack rings by hand, using double strand of thread, stitching in place through the tape, lining, and shade fabric for four or five stitches.

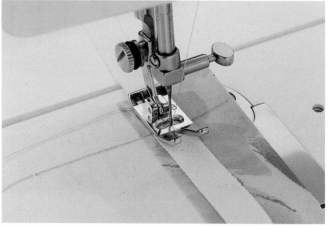

11 Tack the tapes in place at top of shade, matching the last marks on the tapes to marked lines on the shade; do not stitch rings at the top marks.

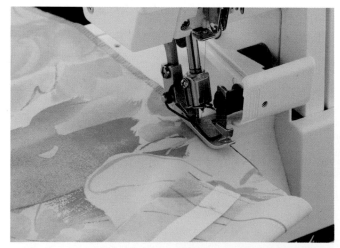

12 Trim excess tapes even with upper edge of shade, and secure ends to shade. Finish upper edge of the shade, using overlock or zigzag stitch; catch the ends of the tapes in the stitching.

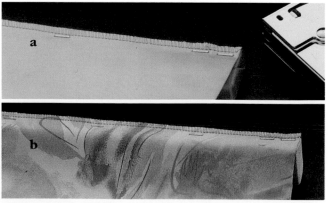

13 Cover mounting board (page 16). Align upper edge of shade to back top edge of mounting board. Staple in place, stapling through the tapes and between them. For inside-mounted shade or outside-mounted shade with 1½" (3.8 cm) projection **(a)**, shade is stapled to wide side of the board. For outside-mounted shade with ¾" (2 cm) projection **(b)**, shade is stapled to narrow side of board.

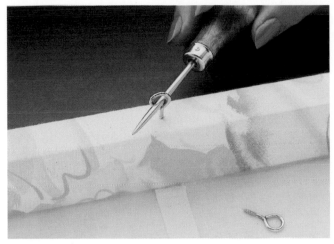

14 Install screw eyes on underside of mounting board, aligning them to rows of rings. For easy installation of screw eyes, use awl or screwdriver as shown.

15 Slide the weight bar into hem at lower edge of shade. Hand-stitch ends of hem closed.

16 Place the shade facedown on a flat surface. Decide whether the draw cord will hang on left or right side of shade. String first row of the shade, opposite the draw side. Run cord through the rings from bottom to top and across the shade through screw eyes; extend cord about three-fourths of the way down the draw side of the shade.

17 Cut and tie the cord for first row securely at bottom ring. String the remaining rows, running the cord through each succeeding row of rings and through the screw eyes; cut and tie each cord at the bottom ring. Apply fabric glue to the knots, to prevent them from fraying or becoming untied.

18 Mount the shade to wall or window frame (page 17). Adjust length of the cords, with shade lowered so the tension on each cord is equal. Tie the cords together just below screw eye. Braid cords to the desired length; knot.

19 Screw awning cleat into window frame or wall. When shade is raised, wrap the cord around awning cleat.

SLATTED
ROMAN SHADES

Slatted Roman shades have a sleek, contemporary look. The flat surface of the shade is interrupted by horizontal pockets that carry narrow wooden slats. Because the slats also give dimensional stability to the shade, only three rows of rings are needed on the back of the shade. For best results, the width of the shade should not exceed 50" (127 cm). As with other styles of Roman shades, the slatted shade is attached to a mounting board and can be installed inside or outside the window frame.

CALCULATING THE POCKET SPACING

It is helpful to make a diagram of the shade, indicating the number of pockets and spaces and labeling the measurements as shown below. The slat pockets and the hem pocket all have a depth of 1½" (3.8 cm). The pockets are evenly spaced, 8" to 10" (20.5 to 25.5 cm) apart, with 9" (23 cm) being most desirable.

For an outside-mounted shade, if the estimated finished length of the shade is not evenly divisible by the desired space between the pockets, the measurement for the finished length can be rounded up until it is, provided there is the necessary wall space above the window for mounting.

If the length of the shade cannot be adjusted, as is the case with an inside-mounted shade that must fit within the window frame, the space between the pockets must be calculated to fit the length. To determine the exact measurement for the spaces, first subtract the 1½" (3.8 cm) hem depth from the finished length. Then divide the remainder by 9, and round this number up or down to the nearest whole number to determine the number of spaces. Next, divide the finished length minus the 1½" (3.8 cm) hem depth by the number of spaces to determine the exact space measurement.

MAKING A DIAGRAM OF THE SHADE

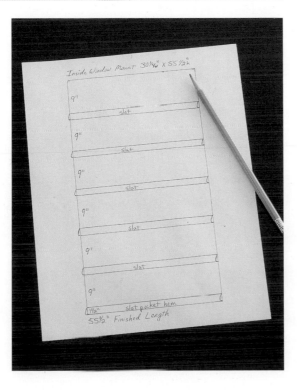

Diagram shade, indicating the necessary number of slat pockets and spaces. Also indicate the hem depth of 1½" (3.8 cm). Label the measurement of all spaces as calculated above. Check to be sure that the total measurement calculated equals the desired finished length of the shade.

MATERIALS

- Decorator fabric.
- Lining fabric.
- Fusible web, ½" (1.3 cm) wide.
- ½" (1.3 cm) plastic rings.
- ⅞" (2.2 cm) wooden slats, such as the slats used for roller shade hem pockets.
- 1 × 2 mounting board, cut to length as determined on page 16.
- Three screw eyes.
- Shade cord.
- Awning cleat.
- 1½" (3.8 cm) angle irons with flat-head screws, for installing an outside-mounted shade.
- 8 × 2½" (6.5 cm) flat-head screws, for installing outside-mounted shade into wall studs; or molly bolts or toggle anchors, for installing outside-mounted shade into drywall or plaster.
- 8 × 1½" (3.8 cm) round-head screws, for installing an inside mounted shade.
- Staple gun and staples.
- Drill and ⅛" drill bit.

CUTTING DIRECTIONS

Determine the finished length of the shade from the top of the mounting board to either the sill or ½" (1.3 cm) below the bottom of the apron.

Determine the finished width of the shade. For an outside mount, the shade should extend at least 1" (2.5 cm) beyond the window frame on each side. For an inside mount, measure the inside of the window frame, from side to side, at the top, middle, and bottom, subtract ⅛" (3 mm) from the narrowest of these measurements for the finished width of the shade.

Cut the shade fabric to the finished length of the shade plus 2" (5 cm) for the turn-under and hem allowance plus 3" (7.5 cm) for each slat pocket plus 4" (10 cm). The cut width is equal to the finished width of the shade plus 3" (7.5 cm) for side hems.

Cut the lining 2" (5 cm) shorter than the cut length of the shade fabric. The cut width of the lining is equal to the finished width of the shade.

Cut a wooden slat for each pocket and one for the hem, ½" (1.3 cm) shorter than the finished width of the shade.

Cut the fabric to cover the mounting board (page 16).

1 Follow steps 1 to 3 on pages 26 and 27. Press under ½" (1.3 cm) at lower edge; then press under 1½" (3.8 cm), to make hem pocket. Stitch close to first fold.

2 Place shade faceup on flat surface. Measure from the lower edge an amount equal to the calculated spacing between pockets plus 3" (7.5 cm). Draw a chalk line parallel to lower edge.

3 Measure up from first marked line the same distance as in step 2, and mark another line. Repeat for each slat pocket.

4 Fold shade, wrong sides together, along first chalk line, keeping the lining and shade fabric together; press. Pin along pressed fold.

5 Repeat step 4 for each marked line. Stitch 1½" (3.8 cm) from foldlines to make slat pockets. Press the pockets toward lower edge of shade.

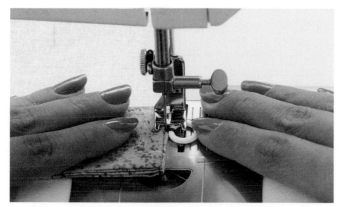

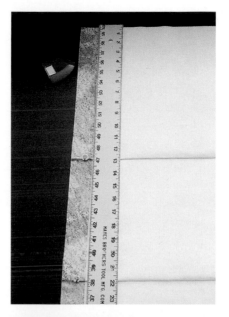

6 Mark placement for rings on wrong side of the shade in three evenly spaced vertical rows, with outer rows 1" (2.5 cm) from the outer edges of the shade. Mark the placement for the bottom rings at upper edge of the hem; mark the placement for remaining rings just under stitching lines. Attach rings by machine or by hand (page 28), keeping slat pockets free.

7 Cover the mounting board (page 16). Place the shade facedown on flat surface. Measure from the lower edge of shade to desired finished length; mark a line on the lining fabric. This may change the length of the top spacing slightly, but ensures that the shade is the correct length.

8 **Inside mount.** Place mounting board flat on shade, aligning lower edge of board to marked line. Mark fabric along opposite edge of board, to mark the distance of the projection away from the first line.

8 **Outside mount.** Place the mounting board on shade, aligning the lower edge of board to marked line. For 1½" (3.8 cm) projection **(a)**, place board flat; for ¾" (2 cm) projection **(b)**, stand board on edge. Mark the fabric as in step 8, left.

9 Cut off excess fabric above second line. Finish upper edge of shade, using overlock or zigzag stitch. Secure shade to the mounting board and install screw eyes as on pages 28 and 29, steps 13 and 14.

10 Slide wooden slats into hem pocket and slat pockets. Hand-stitch ends of pockets closed. Complete the shade as on page 29, steps 16 to 19.

FABRIC ROLLER SHADES

Fabric roller shades not only meet the basic needs of privacy and light control, they also blend well into any decorating scheme.

Interesting effects can be created with the application of lace cutouts or by varying the shape at the lower edge of the shade.

This style of roller shade, with a free-hanging lining, allows the use of almost any fabric. To protect the shade from fading and give a uniform white appearance from the outside of the house, use a standard drapery lining; to also provide total light control, use a blackout lining. For filtered sunlight, make the shade from a lightweight fabric without a lining.

For the best light control and energy efficiency, install the shade inside the window frame. If the window frame is not deep enough to accommodate the roller, mount the brackets on the window frame or just beyond the frame on the wall.

Pulley-system roller shades are easily raised and lowered to the desired height by pulling on a cord loop at the side of the shade. These shades can be made from kits that contain the necessary roller, pulley mechanism, brackets, and hem stick. The instructions that follow may be used for any brand, but may differ from those provided with the kit you purchase.

Shaped lower edges, such as those shown here, add interest to fabric roller shades. Shades may also be embellished with trims (right) or with lace cutouts (opposite).

Pulley-system roller shades *are raised and lowered by pulling on a cord loop at the side. The shades may be made with a free-hanging lining.*

MATERIALS

- Pulley-system roller shade kit that includes adjustable roller, pulley with cord, end plug, and hem stick.
- Fusible web, 3⁄8" and 3⁄4" (1 and 2 cm) wide; masking tape.
- Decorator fabric.
- Drapery lining.
- Lace appliqué, for lace cutout shade.
- Decorative trims, such as gimp or cording, for optional variations at lower edge.

CUTTING DIRECTIONS

Install the mounting brackets and roller; measure the roller as on page 36, step 1, to determine the finished width of the shade. Using a T-square to ensure perfectly squared corners, cut the shade fabric 1½" (3.8 cm) wider than the desired finished width of the shade and 12" (30.5 cm) longer than the desired finished length. For a lined shade, cut the lining 1" (2.5 cm) narrower than the finished width of the shade and 12" (30.5 cm) longer than the finished length.

HOW TO MAKE A FABRIC ROLLER SHADE

1 Install shade brackets, pulley, end plug, and roller according to the manufacturer's instructions. Measure the roller from inner edge of pulley to inner edge of end plug to determine finished width of the shade. Cut fabric (page 35).

2 Turn under and press ¾" (2 cm) on sides of the fabric; fuse in place, using ¾" (2 cm) strip of fusible web. Turn under 2" (5 cm) at the lower edge, for hem-stick pocket; fuse the upper edge of hem-stick pocket in place, using ⅜" (1 cm) strip of fusible web. For an unlined shade, omit step 3.

3 Finish the sides of lining, using overlock or zigzag stitch. Place lining on shade fabric, wrong sides together, with upper edges matching and with shade fabric extending ½" (1.3 cm) beyond lining on each side; pin upper edges together. Check to see that lining hangs squarely centered on shade fabric. Stitch ¼" (6 mm) from upper edge.

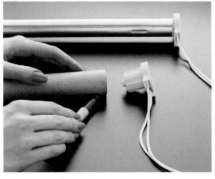

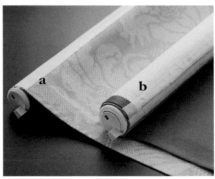

4 Mark a line down the center of a cardboard roller by holding the roller firmly in place on table; place marker flat on the table, and slide it down the length of the roller. If metal roller is used, seam on roller is used instead of a marked line.

5 Attach shade to roller by taping upper edge in place along marked line, from inner edge of the pulley to inner edge of end plug. For a shade that rolls around front of roller **(a)**, tape the shade to roller right side up. For a shade that rolls around back of roller **(b)**, tape the shade to roller wrong side up.

6 Trim hem stick to fit pocket; slide into the pocket. Mount roller shade into brackets. For an unlined shade, omit steps 7 and 8.

7 Mount shade on brackets. Roll shade to the highest position if shade rolls around front of roller **(a)**, allowing lining to extend below the shade hem. Unroll shade to the lowest position if shade rolls around back of the roller **(b)**. Mark lining even with lower edge of shade.

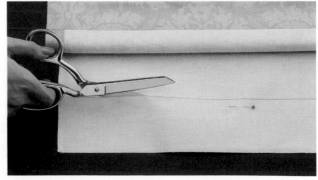

8 Remove shade from brackets. Cut lining ½" (1.3 cm) above marked line. Finish lower edge of lining, using overlock or zigzag stitch. Remount shade.

HOW TO MAKE A ROLLER SHADE WITH A LACE CUTOUT

1 Follow steps 1 and 2, opposite. Pin lace appliqué to shade fabric, right sides up, in desired location. Stitch around outer edge of appliqué, using short, narrow zigzag stitch. (Contrasting thread was used to show detail.)

2 Trim away fabric under appliqué, about ⅛" (3 mm) away from stitches, taking care not to cut the appliqué. For a shade with lining, complete shade as in steps 3 to 8, opposite; for an unlined shade, complete the shade as in steps 4 to 6.

HOW TO MAKE A ROLLER SHADE WITH A SHAPED HEM

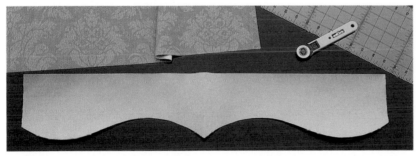

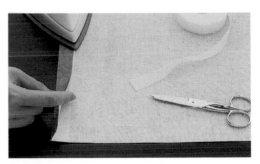

1 Determine finished width of shade as in step 1, opposite. On paper, draw desired symmetrical shape for lower edge of shade. Cut shade fabric as on page 35, cut lining, if desired. Cut fabric for facing 1½" (3.8 cm) wider than finished width of shade; the cut length of facing is 5" to 7" (12.5 to 18 cm), depending on the depth of shaped design.

2 Turn under and press ¾" (2 cm) on sides of the shade fabric and facing; fuse in place, using a ¾" (2 cm) strip of fusible web.

3 Trace the shape for the lower edge of the shade onto wrong side of the facing strip, with longest points of the design ½" (1.3 cm) from the lower edge of the facing. Pin facing strip to the shade fabric, right sides together, aligning the sides and lower edges.

4 Stitch along the marked design line. Trim excess fabric at the lower edge within ¼" (6 mm) of stitching line. Clip to stitching on the curves, and trim corners. Turn the facing to wrong side of the shade; press. Fuse the upper and side edges of facing in place, using ⅜" (1 cm) strip of fusible web.

5 Pin-mark upper edge of facing on sides of shade. Mark line on front of shade, 1½" (3.8 cm) above pin marks, using chalk. Fold shade wrong sides together along marked line; press and pin. Stitch 1½" (3.8 cm) from pressed fold, to make hem-stick pocket. Press pocket toward lower edge of shade.

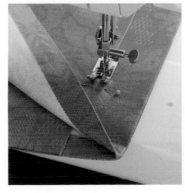

6 Apply decorative trim to lower edge, if desired, using fabric glue or hand stitching. Wrap ends of the trim to wrong side of the shade; secure. For a shade with a lining, complete the shade as in steps 3 to 8, opposite; for an unlined shade, complete shade as in steps 4 to 6.

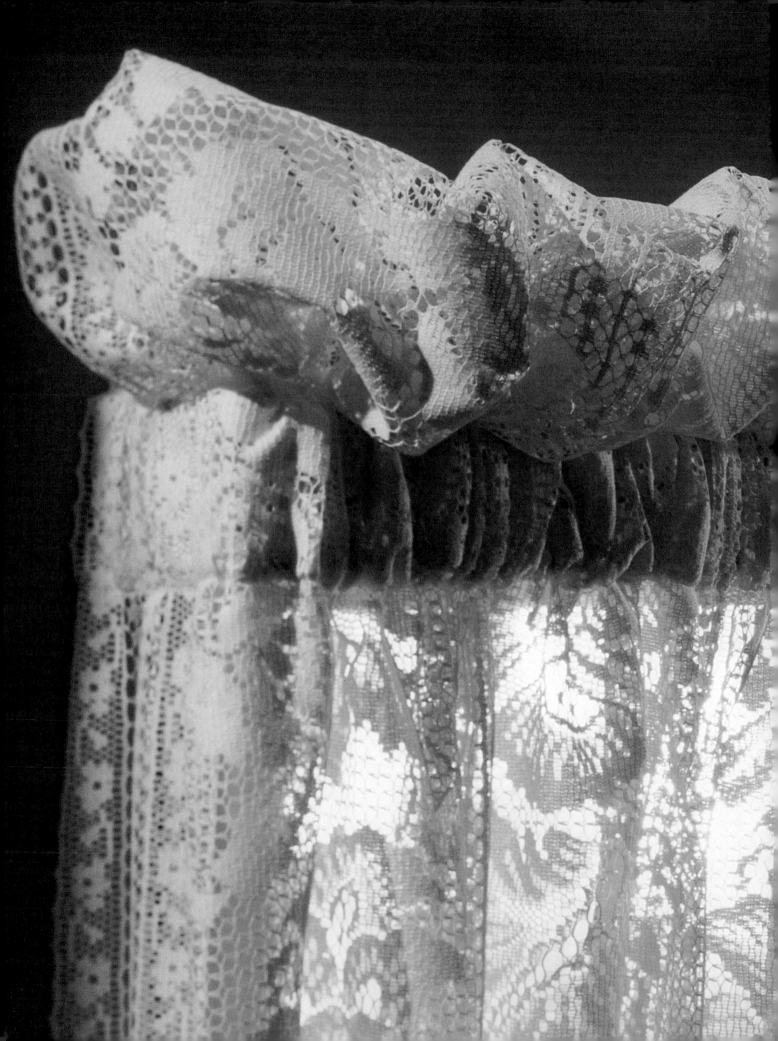

ROD-POCKET BASICS

Rod-pocket curtains are often the choice when selecting a stationary window treatment that is stylish and easy to sew. Many different looks can be achieved with rod-pocket curtains, including interesting variations for headings (pages 44 and 45) and ruffles (page 50).

Several types of rods may be used for rod-pocket curtains, including flat rods in widths of 1", 2½", and 4½" (2.5, 6.5, and 11.5 cm). Wood and metal pole sets, used with elbows or finials, may also be used and are available in several diameters. Poles can also be created, using PVC pipe and fittings as on page 13.

When a pole set with elbows is used, the outer edges of the curtain panels wrap around the elbows to the wall. For curtains mounted on poles with finials, returns can be created by making an opening in the front of the rod-pocket for inserting the pole.

Unlined rod-pocket curtains can be made from sheers or laces, creating a lightweight treatment that allows filtered light to enter the room. For curtains made from mediumweight to heavyweight decorator fabrics, lining is used to make the curtains more durable, add extra body, and support the side hems and headings.

Before cutting the fabric, decide where the window treatment should be positioned and install the curtain rod or pole. Measure from the lower edge of the rod to where you want the lower edge of the curtain. To determine the finished length of the curtain, add the desired depth of the heading and rod pocket to this measurement. This is the finished length of the curtain panel from the top of the heading to the hemmed lower edge.

MATERIALS

- Decorator fabric.
- Lining fabric, optional.
- Drapery weights.
- Curtain rod or pole set with finials or elbows.
- Wooden brackets, keyhole brackets, or elbow brackets, for mounting pole.

TERMS TO KNOW

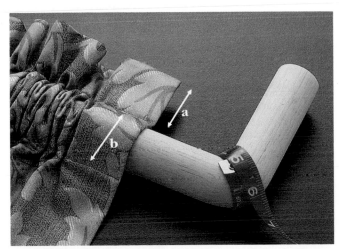

Heading (a) is the portion at the top of a rod-pocket curtain that forms a ruffle when the curtain is on the rod. The depth of the heading is the distance from the top of the finished curtain to the top stitching line of the rod pocket.

Rod pocket (b) is the portion of the curtain where the curtain rod or pole is inserted; stitching lines at the top and bottom of the rod pocket keep the rod in place. To determine the depth of the rod pocket, measure around the widest part of the rod or pole; add ½" (1.3 cm) ease to this measurement, and divide by two.

Returns can be created for rod-pocket curtains that are mounted on poles with finials. The pole is inserted through an opening in the front of the rod pocket, allowing the side of the curtain to return to the wall.

Determine the depth of the rod pocket and heading (page 41) and the depth of the hem at the lower edge. A 4" (10 cm) double-fold hem is often used for the decorator fabric; if the curtain is lined, a 2" (5 cm) double-fold hem is used for the lining.

The cut length of the decorator fabric is equal to the desired finished length of the curtain plus the depth of the heading and the rod pocket plus ½" (1.3 cm) for turn-under at the upper edge plus twice the depth of the hem.

The cut width of the decorator fabric is determined by the length of the curtain rod, including the returns, multiplied by the amount of fullness desired in the curtain.

For sheer fabrics, allow two-and-one-half to three times the length of the rod for fullness; for heavier fabrics, allow two to two-and-one-half times. After multiplying the length of the rod times the desired fullness, divide this number by the number of panels being used for the treatment; add 6" (15 cm) for each panel to allow for 1½" (3.8 cm) double-fold side hems. If it is necessary to piece fabric widths together to make each panel, also add 1" (2.5 cm) for each seam.

Cut the lining fabric 5" (12.5 cm) shorter than the decorator fabric; the cut width of the lining is the same as the decorator fabric.

HOW TO SEW UNLINED ROD-POCKET CURTAINS

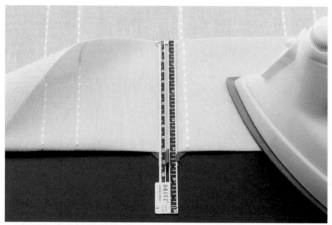

1 Seam fabric widths, if necessary, for each curtain panel. At lower edge, press under an amount equal to the hem depth; repeat to press under a double-fold hem. Stitch, using straight stitch or blindstitch.

2 Press under 1½" (3.8 cm) twice on sides. Tack drapery weights inside the side hems, about 3" (7.5 cm) from lower edge. Stitch to make double-fold hems.

3 Press under ½" (1.3 cm) on upper edge. Then press under an amount equal to rod-pocket depth plus heading depth. If curtains will be mounted on pole with elbow returns, omit steps 4 to 6.

4 Mount rod on wooden, keyhole, or elbow bracket. Measure distance from the wall to center of the pole, as indicated by arrow.

5 Unfold upper edge of curtain on return side of panel. On right side of fabric, measure from the hemmed edge of curtain a distance equal to the measurement in step 4; mark at center of rod pocket. If curtains will be mounted on rod with keyhole brackets, omit step 6.

6 Cut 1" (2.5 cm) strip of fusible interfacing, 1" (2.5 cm) longer than depth of the rod pocket, if the curtains will be mounted on a pole with wooden brackets. Fuse strip to wrong side of curtain panel, centering it directly under mark in step 5. On right side of panel, stitch a buttonhole at the mark, from top to bottom of rod pocket. Refold upper edge of panel along pressed lines; pin.

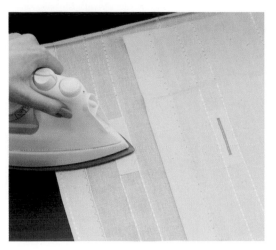

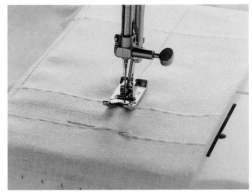

7 Stitch close to first fold; stitch again at depth of heading, using tape on bed of sewing machine as stitching guide.

HOW TO SEW LINED ROD-POCKET CURTAINS

1 Follow step 1, opposite. Repeat for the lining, pressing under and stitching a 2" (5 cm) double-fold hem in the lining.

2 Place curtain panel and lining panel wrong sides together, matching the raw edges at the sides and upper edge; pin. At the bottom, the lining panel will be 1" (2.5 cm) shorter than curtain panel. Complete the curtain as on page 42, steps 2 through 7, handling decorator fabric and lining as one fabric.

HOW TO INSTALL ROD-POCKET CURTAINS

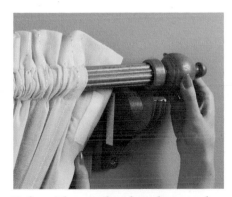

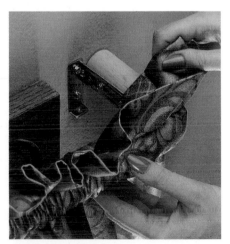

Pole with wooden brackets and finials. Remove the finials; insert pole into rod pocket with ends of the pole extending through the buttonholes. Reattach finials; mount pole. Secure return to the wooden bracket, using self-adhesive hook and loop tape.

Pole with keyhole bracket and finials. Slit center of the rod pocket at point marked in step 5, opposite. Insert pole into rod pocket. Pull return over end of pole, aligning slit to finial screw hole; attach finials through slits, and mount pole. Attach a pin-on ring to inner edge of return, and secure to a tenter hook or cup hook in wall.

Pole with elbows. Insert the pole through the rod pocket; pull the curtain back to expose small screws. Mount the pole on brackets. Slide the curtain over brackets.

DECORATIVE HEADINGS

Flounce heading *drapes down over the front of the rod pocket, creating a mock valance. Allow a heading depth of 12"
to 16" (30.5 to 40.5 cm). This treatment is suitable only for rods or poles with elbow returns. Sheer fabric may be used
for this style in unlined curtains.*

Popped heading *is created by pulling the layers of the heading apart after inserting the rod into the pocket. Allow a
heading depth of 6" to 8" (15 to 20.5 cm); do not press the upper edge of the curtain when turning under the heading
and rod-pocket depth. This style may be used for sheer to mediumweight fabrics and may be lined or unlined.*

Some simple variations in the headings of rod-pocket curtains can dramatically change their look. For some styles, such as the flounce heading or the popped heading, the variation is achieved by simply increasing the depth of the heading and arranging it after it has been installed. For styles such as the contrasting flounce and the welted heading, a separate facing is seamed to the curtain at the top of the heading. Although the instructions that follow are for lined curtains, the lining may be omitted, if desired, depending on the style of the curtain and the fabric selected.

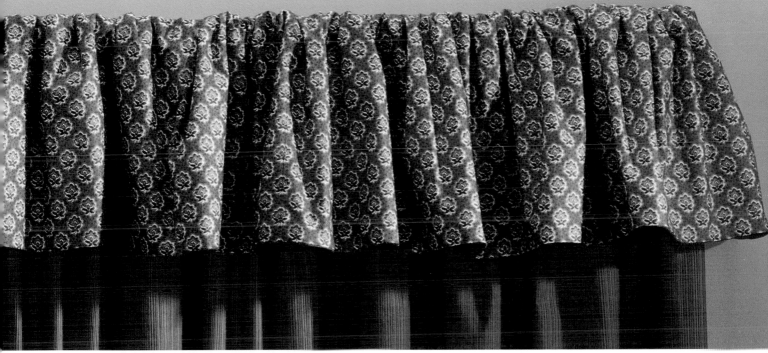

Contrasting flounce *can repeat a fabric that is used in the tieback for a coordinated look. A separate facing of contrasting fabric is sewn to the curtain at the top of the heading. Lining adds body to the heading and prevents show-through when a light-colored fabric is used for the flounce.*

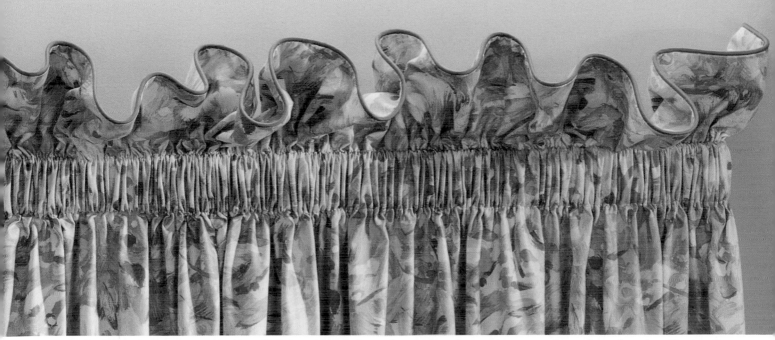

Welted heading, *measuring 4" to 6" (10 to 15 cm) deep, droops into dramatic curves above the rod pocket. Contrasting welting is sewn into the seam at the top of the heading between the curtain and the facing. This style is appropriate for mediumweight fabrics and should always be lined.*

HOW TO MAKE ROD-POCKET CURTAINS WITH A FLOUNCE OR POPPED HEADING

MATERIALS

- Decorator fabric; lining.
- Drapery weights.
- Curtain rod or pole with elbow returns.

CUTTING DIRECTIONS

Cut the decorator fabric and lining as on page 42; allow for a 12" to 16" (30.5 to 40.5 cm) flounce heading, or a 6" to 8" (15 to 20.5 cm) popped heading.

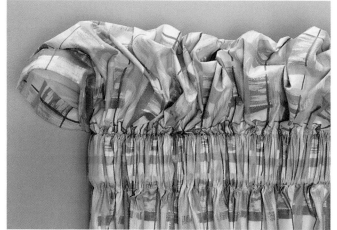

Flounce heading. Sew curtains as on pages 42 and 43. When installing the curtains, drape the heading toward the front, over the rod pocket, and arrange the gathers.

Popped heading. Sew curtains as on pages 42 and 43. Pull layers of heading apart, for a soft, rounded look.

HOW TO MAKE ROD-POCKET CURTAINS WITH A CONTRASTING FLOUNCE

MATERIALS

- Decorator fabric.
- Contrasting decorator fabric, for facing.
- Lining.
- Drapery weights.
- Curtain rod or pole with elbow returns.

CUTTING DIRECTIONS

Cut the decorator fabric for the curtains with the length equal to the desired finished length of the curtains from the top of the curtain rod to the lower edge of the finished curtain plus twice the depth of the hem plus ½" (1.3 cm) for the seam allowance at the top plus the depth of the flounce heading; allow for a 12" to 16" (30.5 to 40.5 cm) flounce heading. Determine the cut width as on page 42.

Cut the fabric for the facing with the length equal to the depth of the heading plus the depth of the rod pocket plus 1" (2.5 cm) for turn-under and seam allowance. The cut width of the facing is the same as the cut width of the decorator fabric.

Cut the lining fabric 5" (12.5 cm) shorter than the decorator fabric. The cut width of the lining is the same as the cut width of the decorator fabric.

1 Seam decorator fabric widths, if necessary, for each curtain panel; repeat for facing and lining panels. At lower edge of curtain panel, press under 4" (10 cm) twice to wrong side; stitch to make double-fold hem. Repeat for hem on lining panel, pressing under 2" (5 cm) twice.

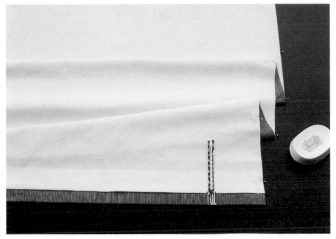

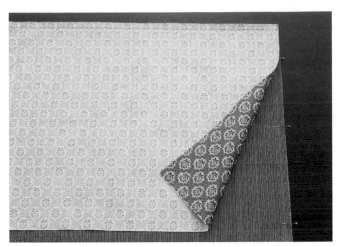

2 Place the curtain panel and the lining panel wrong sides together, matching the raw edges at sides and upper edge; pin. At the bottom, lining panel will be 1" (2.5 cm) shorter than the curtain panel.

3 Pin facing to top of curtain panel, right sides together; if the facing fabric has one-way design, pin the flounce so design is upside down at the upper edge of the curtain panel. Stitch ½" (1.3 cm) seam; press the seam open.

4 Press under 1½" (3.8 cm) twice on sides, folding lining and curtain fabric as one. Open out hem, and trim seam allowance in hem area. Tack drapery weights inside the side hems, about 3" (7.5 cm) from the lower edge. Stitch to make double-fold hems.

5 Press under ½" (1.3 cm) on lower edge of flounce. Turn under facing along seamline; press. Pin flounce to the curtain panel along the lower pressed edge. Mark upper stitching line for rod pocket on facing. Pin along line to keep all layers together.

6 Stitch close to lower pressed edge; stitch again along the marked line, creating rod pocket.

7 Insert the rod or pole through rod pocket, gathering fabric evenly. Mount the rod or pole on brackets, draping heading toward the front, over the rod pocket, and arrange the gathers.

HOW TO MAKE ROD-POCKET CURTAINS WITH A WELTED HEADING

MATERIALS

- Decorator fabric for curtain and facing.
- Contrasting fabric and ¼" (6 mm) cording, for covered welting.
- Lining fabric.
- Drapery weights.
- Curtain rod or pole set.

CUTTING DIRECTIONS

Cut the decorator fabric, facing, and lining as for rod-pocket curtains with a contrasting flounce (page 46); allow for a 4" to 6" (10 to 15 cm) heading. From contrasting fabric, cut bias fabric strips, 2" (5 cm) wide, to cover the cording for the welting.

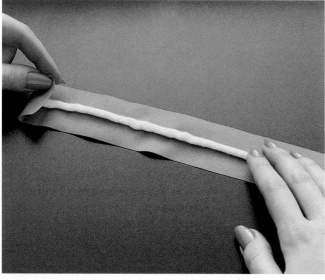

1 Seam the bias fabric strips together. Center the cording on the wrong side of the fabric strip, with the end of cording 1" (2.5 cm) from the end of strip; fold end of the strip back over the cording.

2 Fold the fabric strip around the cording, wrong sides together, matching the raw edges and encasing the end of the cording.

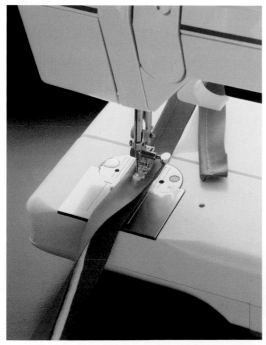

3 Machine-baste close to the cording, using a zipper foot, to create welting.

4 Follow steps 1 and 2 on pages 46 and 47 for contrasting flounce. Stitch the welting to the right side of curtain panel at the upper edge, matching raw edges and stitching over the previous stitches; place encased end of welting 3" (7.5 cm) from side of panel. Stop stitching 5" (12.5 cm) from the opposite side of the panel.

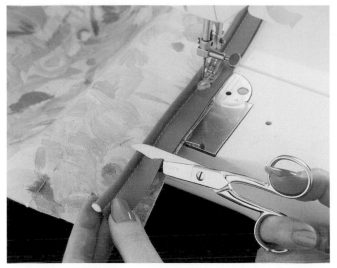

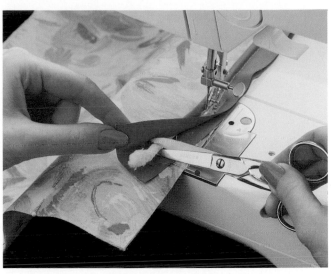

5 Mark the upper edge of the curtain 3" (7.5 cm) from the side; cut the welting 1" (2.5 cm) beyond the mark.

6 Remove the stitching from end of welting, and cut the cording even with the mark on curtain panel.

7 Fold the end of fabric strip over the cording, encasing the end of the cording. Finish stitching welting to the curtain panel, ending 3" (7.5 cm) from the side.

8 Follow steps 3 and 4 on page 47 for the contrasting flounce. When stitching side hems, stitch up to welting and secure threads; start stitching again on other side of the welting.

9 Complete the curtains as on page 47, steps 5 and 6. Insert the rod or pole through the rod pocket, gathering the fabric evenly. Mount the rod or pole on brackets; arrange the heading in deep curves as desired.

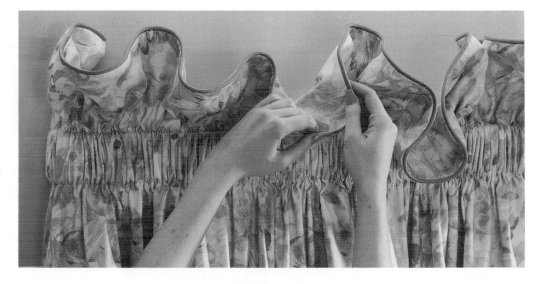

Double ruffle (above) is featured on these tieback curtains, along with ruffled tiebacks (page 55). The ruffles extend only to the bottom of the rod pocket, which allows the shirred fabric to continue uninterrupted across the top of the curtains.

Single ruffle (left) in a contrasting fabric trims this single-panel curtain. The ruffle extends to the top of the heading.

CREATIVE ROD-POCKET CURTAINS

Ruffled curtains add coziness and charm to a room, blending well into various decorating schemes. Deep ruffles on full curtains are romantic and frilly, while narrow ruffles that define the edge of a damask panel are elegant. For a uniform look, make the ruffle from the same fabric as the curtain. Or use a contrasting fabric for the ruffle, perhaps repeating the fabric on ruffled tiebacks (page 55).

Choose from either single or double ruffles. In the method for double ruffles, bulk is eliminated at the seamline, for easier sewing and softer gathers. With both styles, the ruffles are self-faced and sewn into the seam between the curtain fabric and the lining. They are applied to the inner and lower edges of the curtain, curving around the rounded corners of the curtain panels.

For two panels that meet in the center and tie back, begin the ruffle just under the rod pocket on each panel, allowing for an uninterrupted heading across the curtain rod. For separated side panels or a single panel tied to one side, begin the ruffle at the top of the heading.

MATERIALS

- Decorator fabric, for curtain panels.
- Matching or contrasting fabric, for the ruffle.
- Lining fabric.
- Drapery weights.
- Curtain rod.

HOW TO MAKE ROD-POCKET CURTAINS WITH A SINGLE RUFFLE

CUTTING DIRECTIONS

Determine the desired finished length of the curtain, from the top of the heading to the lower edge of the ruffle. Cut the decorator fabric for each curtain panel with the cut length equal to the desired finished length of the curtain minus the finished width of the ruffle, plus the depth of the heading and rod pocket, plus 1" (2.5 cm) for seam allowance and turn-under.

Determine the cut width of each curtain panel by multiplying the length of the rod times the desired fullness (page 19); divide this number by the number of panels being used for the treatment, and add 3½" (9 cm) for each panel to allow for a 1½" (3.8 cm) double-fold

hem on the return side of the panel plus ½" (1.3 cm) for the seam on the ruffled side. If it is necessary to piece fabric widths together to make each panel, also add 1" (2.5 cm) for each seam.

Cut the lining for each panel to the same length and width as the decorator fabric.

For the ruffles, cut fabric strips on the crosswise grain, with the width of the strips equal to twice the desired finished width of the ruffle plus 1" (2.5 cm). Cut as many strips as necessary for a combined length of two to two-and-one-half times the length to be ruffled.

1 Stitch the fabric strips for the ruffle together in ¼" (6 mm) seams, right sides together. Press seams open. Fold ends of strips in half lengthwise, right sides together; stitch across the ends in ¼" (6 mm) seams. Turn right side out, and fold strip in half lengthwise, matching raw edges; press foldline and ends of ruffle strip.

2 Zigzag over a cord on back side of ruffle strip within ½" (1.3 cm) seam allowance, stitching through both layers of ruffle strip.

(Continued)

3 Seam the fabric widths and lining widths, if necessary, for each panel. Curve inside lower edge of one curtain panel by drawing an arc with pencil and string from a pivot point 12" (30.5 cm) up from the bottom and in from the side.

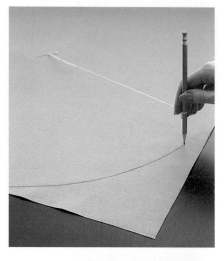

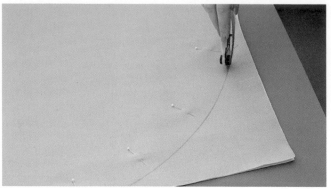

4 Place curtain panel over lining, wrong sides together, matching edges; cut curve along marked line through curtain panel and lining. Repeat for the second panel and lining, if any, curving opposite corner.

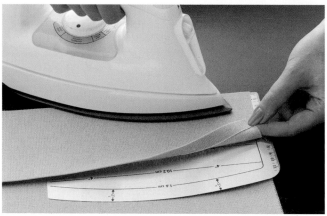

5 Press under ½" (1.3 cm) on the upper edge of curtain panel. Then press under an amount equal to the rod-pocket depth plus heading depth. If you are making a curtain panel with ruffle beginning below the rod pocket, pin-mark location of lower stitching line for rod pocket; unfold pressed edge.

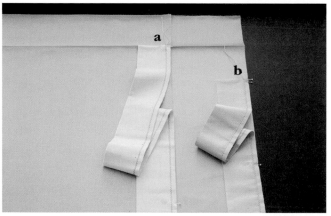

6 Divide ruffle strip into eighths; pin-mark. Divide edges of curtain panel to be ruffled into eighths, beginning at top of heading **(a)** or at lower stitching line of rod pocket **(b)** and ending on lower edge 3" (7.5 cm) from raw edge on return side of panel. Pin ruffle strip to right side of the curtain panel, matching pin marks and raw edges.

7 Pull gathering cord on ruffle to fit edge of the curtain panel; pin in place. Stitch a scant ½" (1.3 cm) from the raw edges.

8 Pin lining to curtain panel, right sides together, matching the raw edges on ruffled side of panel; stitch ½" (1.3 cm) seam on ruffled side.

9 Turn right side out, matching remaining raw edges of curtain panel and lining. Press seam.

10 Press under 1½" (3.8 cm) twice on unruffled side of the curtain panel, folding the curtain fabric and the lining as one. Unfold fabric; tack drapery weight to hem allowance, just above the ruffle. Refold; stitch to make double-fold hem.

11 Refold top of the panel, folding the curtain fabric and lining as one; press. If curtains will be mounted on pole with elbows, follow step 7 on page 43. If curtains will be mounted on pole with finials, follow steps 4 to 7 on pages 42 and 43. Install curtains as on page 43.

HOW TO MAKE ROD-POCKET CURTAINS WITH A DOUBLE RUFFLE

CUTTING DIRECTIONS

Cut the fabric and lining for curtains as on page 51. Determine the desired finished widths of the upper and lower ruffles, with the lower ruffle 1" (2.5 cm) wider than the upper ruffle. Cut fabric strips for each ruffle on the crosswise grain, with the width of the strips equal to twice the desired finished width plus ½" (1.3 cm). Cut as many strips for each ruffle as necessary for a combined length of two to two-and-one-half times the length to be ruffled; seamed fabric strip for upper ruffle must be exactly the same length as seamed strip for the lower ruffle.

1 Stitch the fabric strips for lower ruffle together in ¼" (6 mm) seams, right sides together; press seams open. Repeat for upper ruffle. Press strip for upper ruffle **(a)**, wrong sides together, with raw edge on back side of ruffle strip ½" (1.3 cm) below raw edge on front. Press strip for lower ruffle **(b)**, wrong sides together, with raw edge on front side of ruffle strip ½" (1.3 cm) below raw edge on back.

2 Place upper strip on lower strip, right sides up, matching raw edges of outer layers and inner layers; also match raw edges at short end. Pin the top three layers of fabric together at short end.

3 Fold the unpinned layer of lower ruffle strip around upper ruffle strip; pin in place, with raw edges of top two layers matching. Stitch ¼" (6 mm) seam across short end.

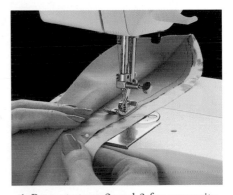

4 Repeat steps 2 and 3 for opposite short end. Turn right side out. Fold back front layer of upper ruffle; pin remaining three layers together, with raw edge of lower layer ½" (1.3 cm) above raw edges of middle layers. Baste ¼" (6 mm) from raw edges of middle layers. Attach ruffle and sew curtains as on pages 51 to 53, steps 2 to 11.

TIEBACKS

Tiebacks are not only functional, they are often the focal point of a window treatment. For a stylish touch, they can be shaped in a gentle curve. Welting can be added to accent the edges of shaped tiebacks, perhaps repeating the detailing of a welted heading (page 45). Ruffled tiebacks are the natural choice for ruffled curtains (page 50), but also work well on curtains with flounce headings (page 44).

Tiebacks are often positioned so they divide the curtain panel vertically into thirds. If the tiebacks are positioned one-third of the way from the bottom of the curtains, more window glass remains covered and the window appears wider. If they are positioned one-third of the way from the top, more window glass

Shaped tiebacks (left and below) have a clean, tailored look. They may be sewn with or without welting.

is revealed and the window appears longer. Also consider where to position the tieback in relation to any window details, such as sills or mullions.

Measure for the finished length of the tiebacks after the curtains are made and installed. Generally, the length of each tieback is one-half the total length of the curtain rod plus the projection of the rod. This allows each curtain panel to be pulled back to one-half its width. To visualize how the curtain will look tied back, wrap a cloth tape measure around the curtain panel at the desired tieback height and pull the panel back the desired distance. Angle the tape measure upward toward the outer edge of the curtain where the tieback holder will be placed.

Ruffled tiebacks (right and below) add a romantic touch. They may have a single or double ruffle.

HOW TO MAKE SHAPED TIEBACKS

MATERIALS

- Decorator fabric.
- Fusible polyester fleece or interfacing.
- Cording, for tiebacks with welting.
- Tieback rings, two for each tieback.
- Tieback holders, one for each tieback.
- Flexible curve or curved ruler.

CUTTING DIRECTIONS

Determine the desired finished length of the tiebacks (page 55). Make the pattern for the tiebacks as in steps 1 to 3, below. For each tieback, cut two pieces of decorator fabric and one piece of fusible fleece or interfacing, using the pattern.

If welting is desired, cut bias fabric strips to cover the welting, with the total length of the seamed strips 2" to 3" (5 to 7.5 cm) longer than the distance around the tieback. To determine the cut width of the strips, wrap a tape measure around the cording; the cut width of the strips is equal to the measurement around the cording plus 1" (2.5 cm).

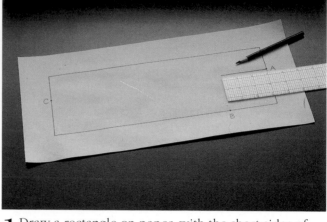

1 Draw a rectangle on paper, with the short sides of the rectangle measuring 5" (12.5 cm); the long sides of the rectangle are equal to one-half the finished length of tieback. Mark Point A on one short side, 3" (7.5 cm) from the lower corner. Mark Point B on the long side 3" (7.5 cm) from the same corner. Mark Point C on the opposite short side, 2" (5 cm) down from upper corner. Draw 3" (7.5 cm) line from Point A parallel to long sides.

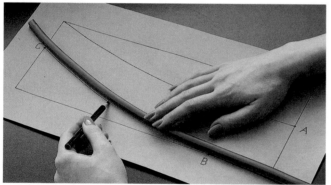

2 Use a flexible curve or a curved ruler to mark a gradual curve for the upper edge of the tieback, connecting the end of the 3" (7.5 cm) line to the upper corner on opposite side of the rectangle. For the lower edge of tieback, draw a curved line from Point C to Point B.

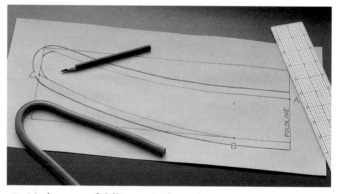

3 Mark center foldline on side with Point A; round corners on the opposite side, for the return. Add ½" (1.3 cm) seam allowances at the upper and lower edges and around the return end.

4 Cut fabric and fusible fleece or interfacing, above. Trim ½" (1.3 cm) from the outer edge of fleece or interfacing; center on wrong side of outer tieback piece, and fuse in place. For tieback without welting, omit steps 5 to 9.

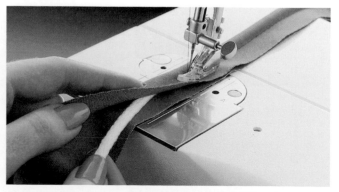

5 Seam bias fabric strips together in ¼" (6 mm) seams. Fold fabric strip over cording, right side out, matching the raw edges. Using zipper foot, machine-baste close to the cording.

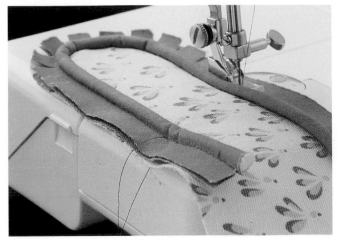

6 Stitch the welting to the right side of tieback, matching raw edges; start 2" (5 cm) from the end of welting in an area of the tieback that will be concealed behind the curtain. To ease welting at the rounded corners, clip seam allowances to basting stitches.

7 Stop stitching 2" (5 cm) from the point where the ends of the welting will meet. Cut off one end of welting so it overlaps the other end by 1" (2.5 cm).

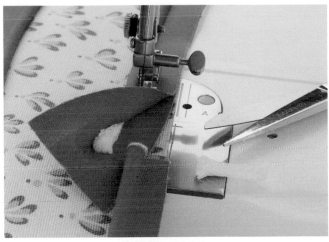

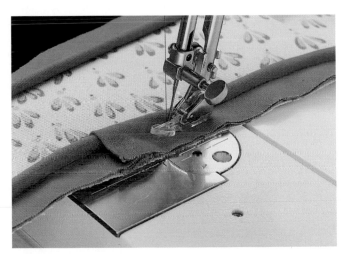

8 Remove the stitching from one end of the welting, and trim the ends of the cording so they just meet.

9 Fold under ½" (1.3 cm) of fabric on overlapping end. Lap it around the other end; finish stitching the welting to the tieback.

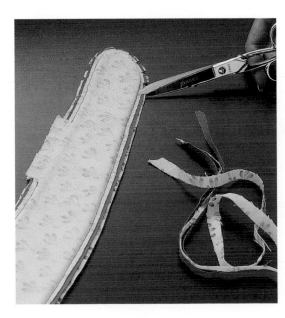

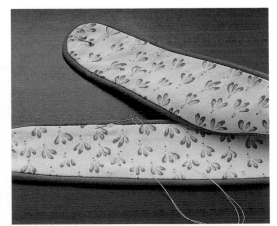

10 Pin the outer tieback and lining pieces right sides together. Stitch ½" (1.3 cm) from raw edges, crowding cording; leave opening for turning. Trim seam allowances. Clip the curved upper and lower edges every ½" (1.3 cm); notch the curves of the return ends.

11 Turn right side out; press. Slipstitch the opening closed. Secure tieback rings to wrong side of tieback, with one ring centered near each end. Attach the tieback to tieback holder (page 10).

HOW TO MAKE RUFFLED TIEBACKS

MATERIALS

• Decorator fabric.

• Fusible interfacing.

• Tieback rings, two for each tieback.

• Tieback holders, one for each tieback.

CUTTING DIRECTIONS

Determine the desired finished length of the tiebacks (page 55). Cut one 3½" (9 cm) fabric strip for each tieback band, with the length of the strip equal to the finished length of the tieback plus 1" (2.5 cm); this gives a finished band width of 1¼" (3.2 cm). Cut a 2½" (6.5 cm) strip of fusible interfacing for each tieback, with the length equal to the finished length of the tieback. Cut the fabric for single or double ruffles as for ruffled curtains on page 51 or 53.

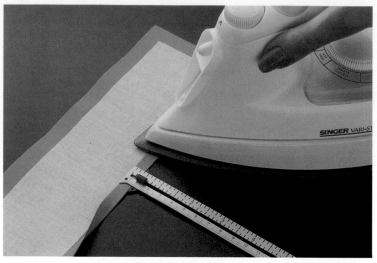

1 Center the interfacing on wrong side of tieback; fuse in place. Press up ⅜" (1 cm) on one long side of tieback.

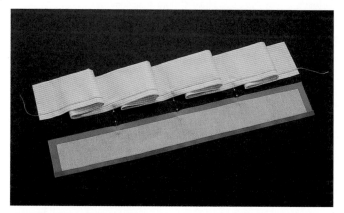

2 Prepare single ruffles as on page 51, steps 1 and 2, or prepare double ruffles as on page 53, steps 1 to 4. Divide ruffle strip and tieback band into fourths; pin-mark.

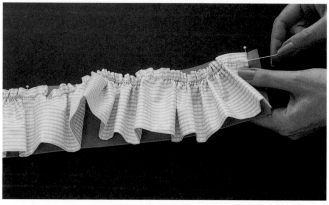

3 Pin the ruffle strip to the unfolded side of the tieback band, right sides together, matching pin marks and raw edges, with ends of ruffle strip ½" (1.3 cm) from ends of the band. Pull up gathering cord on the ruffle to fit band; pin in place. Stitch ½" (1.3 cm) from raw edges.

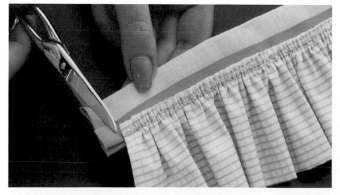

4 Trim seam allowance of the ruffle to ¼" (6 mm). Fold the end of the band in half, wrong sides together, with the folded edge extending ⅛" (3 mm) beyond stitching line. Stitch ½" (1.3 cm) from end, taking care not to catch the ruffle in stitching; trim seam allowances. Repeat for the opposite end.

5 Turn the band right side out, and press; the folded edge extends ⅛" (3 mm) below the stitching line on the back of the band. Pin in place; stitch in the ditch from the right side, catching the folded edge on the back of band. Secure tieback rings as on page 57, step 11; attach the tieback to the tieback holder (page 10).

MORE IDEAS FOR TIEBACKS

Scalloped edge on a shaped tieback adds a designer touch to a window treatment.

Knotted men's necktie, tied in a Windsor knot, holds back a plaid curtain.

Ribbons with floral nosegay gather an hourglass curtain.

Jute rope serves as a creative tieback with rustic appeal.

Scarf used as a tieback has a soft, carefree look.

HOURGLASS CURTAINS

The name for these curtains is derived from their shape. Hourglass curtains are held taut between rods at the top and bottom and drawn in at the center with a tieback, exposing some of the window glass. Often used on French doors, hourglass curtains rest close to the glass, allowing free movement of the door. Hourglass curtains are usually mounted on narrow sash rods, although wide curtain rods can be used for a different look. Spring-tension rods can also be used when the hourglass curtain is mounted inside the window frame. Decorator sheer fabrics are the best choice for this treatment, especially for doors or windows that are viewed from both sides.

Accurate planning and measuring ensure successful results when making hourglass curtains. To visualize the finished curtain, it is helpful to mark the shape of the hourglass on the window or door, using ribbon or twill tape (page 62). The width of the curtain at the tieback should be between one-third and one-half the width of the window treatment at the top and bottom. Whenever possible, the lower edge of the upper rod and the upper edge of the lower rod should clear the glass by at least ½" (1.3 cm). Be sure to allow room for the rod and the desired heading depth at the top and bottom of the curtain.

French doors (opposite) feature hourglass curtains for an elegant look.

Small window has an hourglass curtain from lightweight cotton fabric for a cozy country look.

CREATIVE ROD-POCKET CURTAINS

61

1 Install rods. Tape a strip of ribbon or twill tape to door or window, outlining desired shape of curtain. Begin at lower outside corner of top rod, angling in desired distance to center, and then out to upper outside corner of bottom rod. Repeat for opposite side.

2 Measure width of curtain across top or bottom; this is referred to as Measurement A. Measure width of curtain across center; this is referred to as Measurement B. Subtract Measurement B from Measurement A; record the difference.

3 Measure the length of the ribbon down one angled side; this is referred to as Measurement C. Measure the length of the curtain down the center, measuring from the lower edge of the top rod to the upper edge of the bottom rod; this is referred to as Measurement D. Subtract Measurement D from Measurement C; record the difference.

MATERIALS

- Ribbon or twill tape.
- Sheer to lightweight decorator fabric.
- Two sash rods, curtain rods with up to 1¼" (3.2 cm) projection, or spring-tension rods.
- White heavyweight sew-in interfacing; ivory lightweight fusible interfacing, to prevent show-through, optional.

CUTTING DIRECTIONS

Cut the fabric with the length equal to Measurement C plus four times the rod-pocket depth and four times the desired heading depth (page 41) plus 1" (2.5 cm) for turn-under. The cut width of the fabric is equal to two-and-one-half to three times Measurement A, depending on the desired fullness, plus 4" (10 cm) for 1" (2.5 cm) double-fold side hems. Seam fabric widths together, if necessary, using French seams (page 20).

Cut a strip of fabric for the tieback, with the length equal to two times Measurement B plus 1½" (3.8 cm). The cut width of the fabric strip is equal to twice the desired finished width of the tieback plus 1" (2.5 cm).

Cut one strip each of heavyweight sew-in interfacing and optional ivory lightweight fusible interfacing, with the length 1" (2.5 cm) shorter than the cut length of the tie-back strip; the cut width is ⅛" (3 mm) narrower than the finished width of the tieback. Fuse the strips together.

HOW TO MAKE AN HOURGLASS CURTAIN

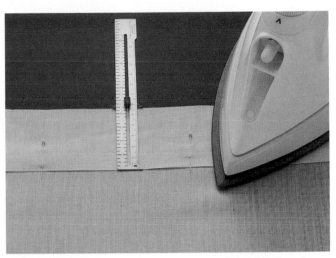

1 Seam fabric widths together, if necessary, using French seams (page 20). Press under 1" (2.5 cm) twice on sides of curtain panel; stitch to make double-fold hems, using straight stitch or blindstitch.

2 Press under ½" (1.3 cm) on upper edge. Then press under an amount equal to the rod-pocket depth plus the heading depth; pin.

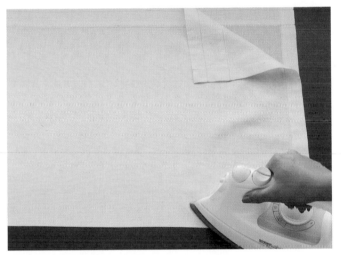

3 Stitch close to the first fold. Stitch again at the depth of the heading.

4 Repeat steps 2 and 3 for lower edge of curtain panel. Fold curtain in half crosswise, right sides together, matching top and bottom rod pockets and headings. Press foldline across center of curtain.

5 Divide the difference between Measurement A and Measurement B in half. Then multiply this number by the amount of fullness allowed for the curtain. Measure this distance along pressed fold from one side toward center; pin-mark. Repeat for opposite side. (See inset.)

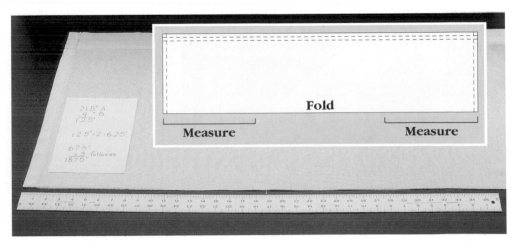

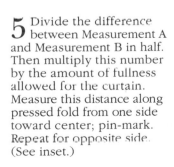

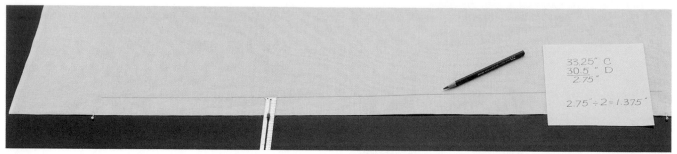

6 Divide the difference between Measurement C and Measurement D in half. Measure in from the fold at pin marks a distance equal to this measurement; mark. Draw a line between pin marks, parallel to the foldline.

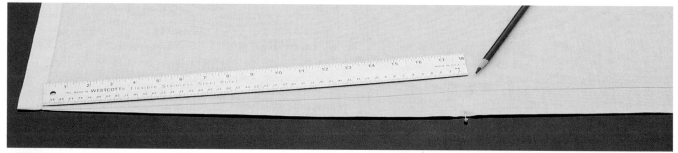

7 Extend line to pressed fold at inner edges of side hems, using straightedge, if sash rods or spring-tension rods are used. If rods have up to a 1¼" (3.2 cm) projection, taper line to 4" (10 cm) from side hems. Stitch on marked line, making a long dart.

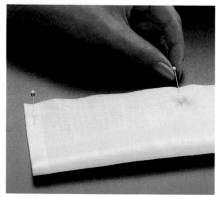

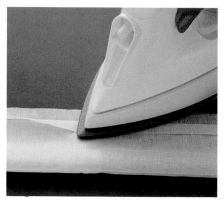

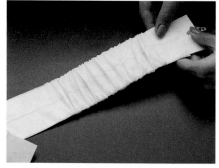

8 Press under ½" (1.3 cm) on one short end of the tieback. Fold the tieback in half lengthwise, right sides together; pin.

9 Sew a ½" (1.3 cm) seam along the length of tieback; press seam open.

10 Turn tieback right side out, using safety pin or bodkin. Center the seam on back of tieback; press. Insert interfacing strip into tieback (optional ivory interfacing faces front).

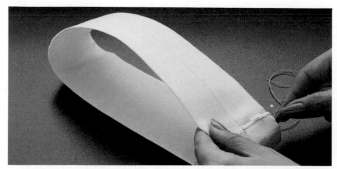

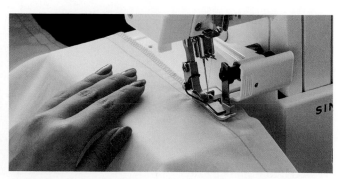

11 Insert unfinished end of tieback into pressed end, overlapping ½" (1.3 cm). Slipstitch ends together, making a circular tieback.

12 Install curtain (opposite); check fit. Adjust stitching of dart, if necessary. Trim fabric ½" (1.3 cm) from stitched dart; finish seam, and press. Reinstall curtain.

HOW TO INSTALL AN HOURGLASS CURTAIN
USING RODS WITH BRACKETS

1 Remove rods from brackets; insert top rod into top rod pocket of curtain. Mount top rod in brackets.

2 Place curtain through tieback. Insert bottom rod into bottom rod pocket.

3 Distribute gathers evenly on rods. Position tieback at center of curtain. Mount bottom rod in brackets, pulling curtain taut.

4 Secure tieback to center of curtain, using concealed safety pin.

HOW TO INSTALL AN HOURGLASS CURTAIN
USING SPRING-TENSION RODS

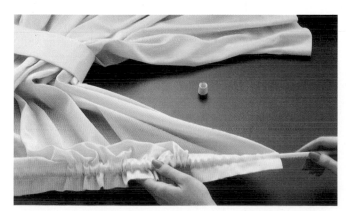

1 Place curtain through tieback. Remove rubber tips from ends of spring-tension rods. Insert the spring-tension rods in top and bottom rod pockets. Replace rubber tips.

2 Mount rods inside window frame, pulling curtain taut between them; distribute gathers evenly, covering the rubber tips of rods. Center tieback over seam. Secure the tieback to center of curtain, using concealed safety pin.

CREATIVE ROD-POCKET CURTAINS

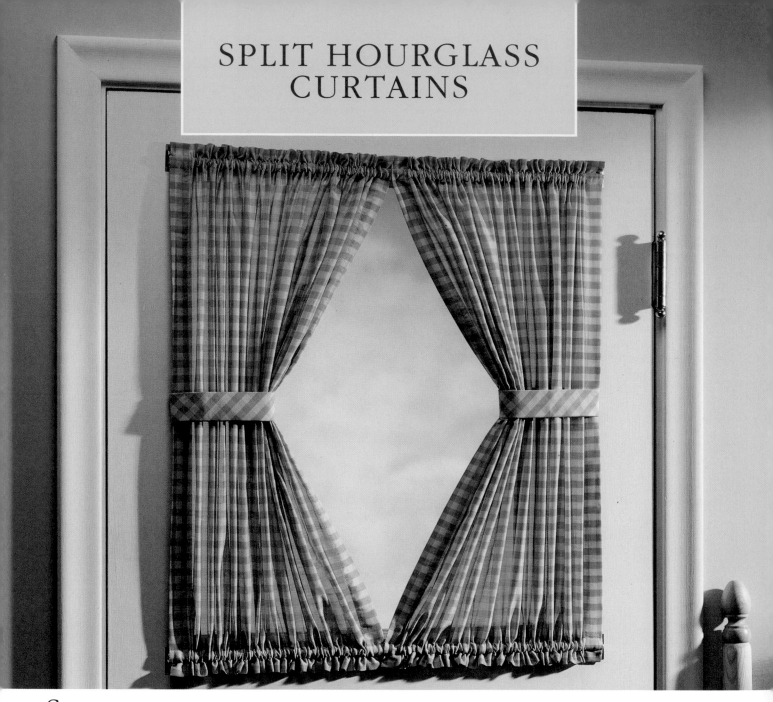

SPLIT HOURGLASS CURTAINS

Split hourglass curtains form a diamond of open glass at the center of the door or window. Like other hourglass curtains, the shaping is achieved by a dart sewn at the center, hidden under the tieback. The split hourglass is made in two panels, shaped in opposite directions and installed on the same rods at the top and bottom.

MATERIALS

- Sheer to lightweight decorator fabric.
- Two sash rods, rods with up to 1¼" (3.2 cm) projection, or spring-tension rods.
- White heavyweight sew-in interfacing.
- Ivory lightweight fusible interfacing, to prevent show-through of white heavyweight interfacing, optional.
- Thumbtacks or self-adhesive hook and loop tape, for securing tiebacks.

CUTTING DIRECTIONS

Cut the fabric for each curtain panel, with the length equal to the angled side measurement as determined in step 2, opposite, plus four times the depth of the rod pocket plus four times the desired heading depth plus 1" (2.5 cm) for turn-under. The cut width of the fabric for each panel is equal to two-and-one-half to three times the finished width of the panel plus 4" (10 cm) to allow for 1" (2.5 cm) double-fold side hems.

Cut a strip of fabric for each tieback, with the length of the strip equal to two times the center width of one panel plus 1½" (3.8 cm). The cut width of the strip is equal to three times the desired finished width of the tieback. Cut the sew-in and optional fusible interfacing as on page 62.

HOW TO MEASURE FOR A SPLIT HOURGLASS CURTAIN

 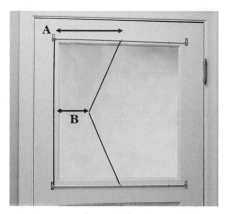 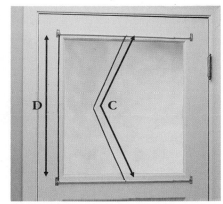

1 Install the rods. Tape a strip of twill tape or ribbon to the window, outlining the desired shape of curtain panels. Begin at lower center of the upper rod, angling out to the desired inner point for tieback, and then in to upper center of the lower rod.

2 Measure the width across top or bottom of one panel; this is referred to as Measurement A. Measure the width of panel across center; this is referred to as Measurement B. Subtract Measurement B from Measurement A; record the difference.

3 Measure length of twill tape or ribbon down angled side; this is referred to as Measurement C. Measure length of curtain down straight side, measuring from lower edge of upper rod to upper edge of lower rod; this is referred to as Measurement D. Subtract Measurement D from Measurement C; record the difference.

HOW TO MAKE A SPLIT HOURGLASS CURTAIN

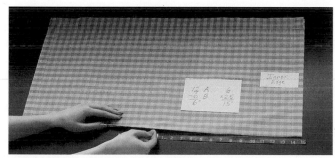 

1 Follow steps 1 to 4 on page 63, for each curtain panel. Multiply the difference between Measurement A and Measurement B, as determined in step 2, above, by the amount of fullness allowed for the curtain. Measure this distance along pressed fold from inner side of the panel toward outer side; pin-mark. Repeat for the second panel.

2 Divide the difference between Measurement C and Measurement D, as determined in step 3, above, in half. Measure from the pressed fold a distance equal to this measurement; draw a line through hemmed edge on outer side to the pin mark, parallel to the foldline.

3 Extend the line from pin mark to pressed fold at hem on inner side of panel; line does not extend into hem allowance. Stitch on marked line, creating a dart through center of each curtain panel. Complete curtain and tiebacks as on page 64, steps 8 to 11.

4 Install curtain as on page 65, steps 1 to 4 for rods with brackets, or steps 1 and 2 for spring-tension rods. Secure tiebacks to outer edges of window frame, using thumbtacks or self-adhesive hook and loop tape. Check fit and finish curtain as on page 64, step 12.

MORE IDEAS FOR HOURGLASS CURTAINS

Angled panels *expose only a small area of glass. The curtains, sewn like single panels of the split hourglass curtain on page 66, are mounted on 1" (2.5 cm) sash rods.*

Hourglass curtain *(below) is stretched horizontally between spring-tension rods in this small window.*

Long tails of ribbon emphasize the high placement of the tieback on this hourglass curtain. This curtain is sewn as on pages 62 to 64, stitching the dart one-third of the way down from the top of the curtain, rather than across the middle.

Triple diamond effect (below) is created by mounting two hourglass curtains (page 61) between two split hourglass panels (page 66). All the panels are mounted on the same tension rods.

Top
Treatments

ROD-POCKET SWAGS

This softly gathered swag valance is a versatile top treatment that can be styled in a variety of ways. For country charm or soft femininity, sew a ruffle to the lower edge. Elegant fabric and bullion fringe (page 77) create a more formal look. The valance can fall in one deep, graceful swag or two swags with equal depths. For yet another look, the valance can be divided to create a triple swag with two equal swags on either side of a third, deeper swag (page 76).

Regardless of the size of the valance or the number of swags, the valance is constructed from a half circle of fabric. Surprisingly, the straight edge of the half circle actually becomes the lower curved edge of the valance to which the ruffle or fringe is attached. The heading and rod pocket of the valance are sewn along the curve of the half circle. To avoid seams, the length of the straight edge should not exceed twice the width of the decorator fabric.

MATERIALS

- Twill tape or ribbon.
- Decorator fabric for valance; the amount needed is equal to the length of the twill tape or ribbon, as determined at right, plus twice the depth of the heading and rod pocket, plus 1" (2.5 cm). Additional fabric is needed for the optional ruffle.

- Lining; the amount needed is equal to the length of the twill tape or ribbon, as determined at right, plus twice the depth of the heading and rod pocket, plus 1" (2.5 cm).
- Curtain rod or pole set.
- Cord, such as pearl cotton, for gathering.

HOW TO MEASURE FOR A ROD-POCKET SWAG

Install the curtain rod or pole. Drape a length of twill tape or ribbon from the rod, simulating the desired shape at the lower edge of the valance. If more than one swag is desired, tie the tape or ribbon into the desired position for each swag. Do not include the width of the ruffle in the depth of the swags. Measuring from the bottom of the rod, measure the length of the twill tape or ribbon.

Rod-pocket swags may have either a single or double ruffle and may have one or two swags, as shown opposite and at right.

HOW TO SEW A SINGLE ROD-POCKET SWAG

Determine the depth of the heading and rod pocket (page 41). Fold the decorator fabric in half crosswise; trim the selvages. Mark an arc, using a straightedge and pencil, measuring from the outer edge at the fold, a distance equal to one-half the measured length of the lower edge of the valance plus the depth of the heading and rod pocket plus ½"

(1.3 cm). Cut on the marked line through both layers. Cut the lining to the same size.

For the ruffle, cut fabric strips on the crosswise grain of the fabric, with the width of the fabric strips equal to twice the desired finished width of the ruffle plus 1" (2.5 cm). Cut as many fabric strips as necessary for a combined length of two to two-and-one-half times the measured length of the twill tape or ribbon (page 73).

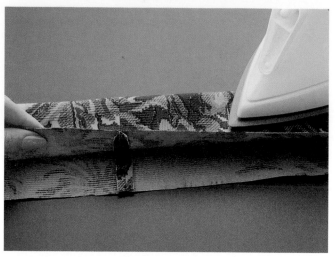

1 Stitch the fabric strips for ruffle together in ¼" (6 mm) seams, right sides together. Press the seams open. Fold ends of strips in half lengthwise, right sides together; stitch across ends in ¼" (6 mm) seams. Turn right side out; press.

2 Zigzag over a cord within ½" (1.3 cm) seam allowance, stitching through both layers of ruffle strip.

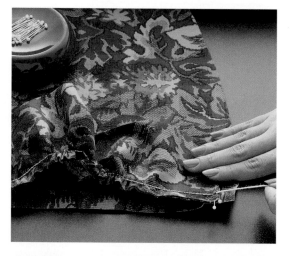

3 Divide ruffle and straight edge of valance into fourths or eighths; pin-mark, placing outer pins of valance ½" (1.3 cm) from raw edges. Pin ruffle along straight edge of the valance, right sides together, matching raw edges and pin marks; pull the cord, gathering fabric to fit between the pins. Stitch ruffle to valance a scant ½" (1.3 cm) from the raw edges.

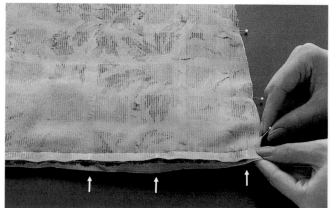

4 Mark ½" (1.3 cm) seam allowance and the depths of heading and rod pocket (page 41) on wrong side of valance fabric (arrows), at each end of straight edge. Pin valance to lining, right sides together, matching raw edges.

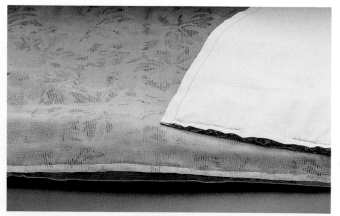

5 Stitch valance to lining in ½" (1.3 cm) seam, stitching with valance faceup. Leave an opening for the rod pocket at each end of the straight edge, and an opening near the center of the straight edge for turning.

6 Press the lining seam allowance toward the lining. Trim the corners diagonally.

7 Turn valance right side out; press seamed edges. Stitch the center opening closed. Mark chalk lines for depth of heading and depth of rod pocket on curved edge of valance. Pin layers together. Stitch on marked lines.

8 Insert the curtain rod or pole into the rod pocket, gathering fabric evenly. Install rod on brackets. Adjust the folds of valance as desired.

HOW TO SEW A DOUBLE ROD-POCKET SWAG

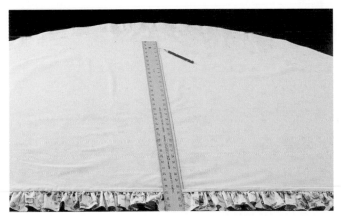

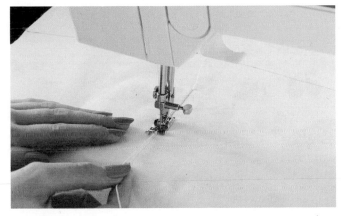

1 Follow steps 1 to 7, opposite. Place valance facedown on flat surface. Divide the lower straight edge, between the rod pockets at ends, into two equal parts; mark ½" (1.3 cm) above seam. Divide upper curved edge into two equal parts. Holding straightedge at marks, draw a line from lower edge, between marks, to a point 2" (5 cm) below the rod pocket.

2 Cut a length of cord, such as pearl cotton, twice the length of the marked line plus 4" (10 cm). Using zigzag stitch of medium length and narrow width, stitch over the cord down left side of line, beginning 2" (5 cm) below the rod pocket, to end of the line; take care not to catch the cord in stitching. Leave needle down in the fabric to right of cord; pivot.

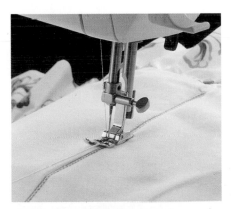

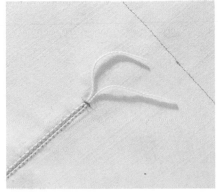

3 Continue stitching over the cord on opposite side of the line toward upper edge, taking care not to catch cord in stitching.

4 Secure stitches at top of line by stitching in place over both cords, using wide zigzag stitch.

5 Follow step 8, above. Draw up gathering cords to desired height; tie cords. Adjust gathers and folds of the valance.

MORE IDEAS FOR ROD-POCKET SWAGS

Single swag (left) without a ruffle is sewn with a popped heading as on page 46. The swag is lined with matching fabric.

Fringe-trimmed swag (opposite) is made from an elegant jacquard fabric for a formal look.

Triple swag (below) is trimmed with tassel fringe instead of a ruffle. The swag has a 2" (5 cm) heading and a 3" (7.5 cm) rod pocket. Follow the steps for a double swag on page 75, except divide the lower straight edge between rod pockets into three parts; also pin-mark upper curved edge about 5" (12.5 cm) from each end, and divide remaining space into three parts. If window sections are unequal, divide spaces for swags in proportion to the window sections.

The simplicity of scarf swags makes them a favorite informal top treatment. In this method, the shaping of the swag is achieved by cutting out wedges of excess fullness from a length of fabric at each point where the swag crosses a swag holder. The swag is then constructed by sewing the angled pieces together and adding a lining. Simply fanfold the swag along the seams and drape it over the swag holders, to make hanging the swag virtually foolproof. Make swags that drape into a single swoop or into multiple swoops, adding poufs at the top of the side panels, if desired. This scarf swag uses the full width of the fabric and can be either self-lined or lined in a contrasting fabric.

Swag holders are available in several styles, including medallions and scarf rings; decorative tieback holders and holdbacks may also be used (page 10). Mount the holders in the desired locations at the top of the window before beginning the project, and measure for the treatment using twill tape.

Scarf swags can be sewn in many variations. Above, a swag with a single swoop is held in place with scarf rings. Below, a swag with multiple swoops drapes over swag holders.

MATERIALS

- Swag holders; one swag holder is needed at each upper corner of the window for a swag with a single swoop, and one holder is needed for each additional swoop.

- Twill tape.

- Decorator fabric for swag, length determined as on page 80, step 1, for swag with single swoop, or as on page 82, step 1, for swag with multiple swoops.

- Matching or contrasting fabric for lining, length equal to decorator fabric.

Scarf swag with poufs (opposite) is an easy variation of a basic swag. To make the poufs, simply add extra length to the side panels; then fold and tie the poufs in place.

TOP TREATMENTS

HOW TO MEASURE FOR A SCARF SWAG
WITH A SINGLE SWOOP

1 Mount swag holders in desired locations. Drape a length of twill tape over the holders as shown, extending to longest points of tapered sides and stretching straight across top of window. This will be the finished length on the upper edge of the swag.

2 Drape a second length of twill tape over the holders as shown, extending to shortest points of tapered sides and dipping to lowest point desired at center of swoop. This will be the finished length on the lower edge of the swag. Mark both tapes at holders.

3 Measure and record the lengths of the tape for each section. Measurement A is from the long point to the holder, Measurement B is from the short point to the holder, Measurement C is the distance straight across between the holders, and Measurement D is the length of the swoop between the holders.

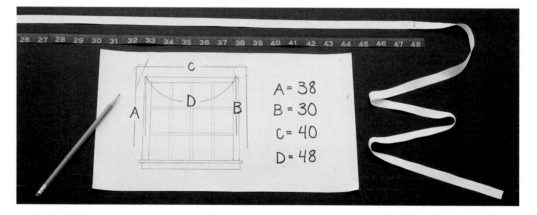

HOW TO MAKE A SCARF SWAG WITH A SINGLE SWOOP

1 Cut the full width of the fabric, with the length equal to Measurement D plus two times Measurement A plus 3" (7.5 cm) for seam allowances. Measure from each end of the fabric a distance equal to Measurement A plus 1" (2.5 cm). Cut the fabric perpendicular to the selvage at these points.

2 Turn one end piece completely around, if using fabric with an obvious one-way design, so upward direction on both ends points toward the middle; when hung, the design will face in correct direction on end pieces. Label tops of each end piece.

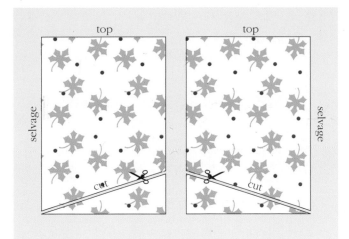

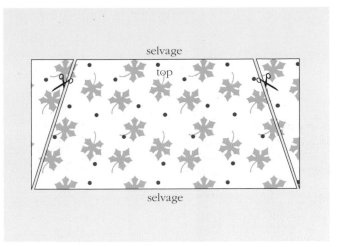

3 Subtract Measurement B from Measurement A. Mark a point on the inside edge of one end piece this distance from the lower cut edge. Draw a line from this point to lower outside corner; cut away triangular wedge. Repeat for other end piece, cutting angle in opposite direction.

4 Subtract Measurement C from Measurement D; divide this measurement in half. Mark a point on upper edge of the center piece this distance from outer edge. Draw a line from this point to lower corner; cut away triangular wedge. Repeat for opposite side of center piece.

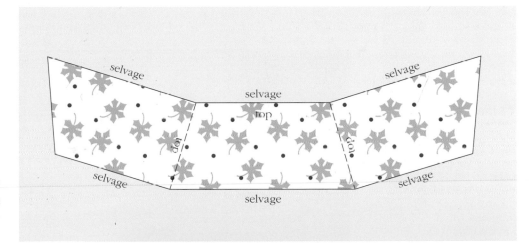

5 Cut lining, using swag pieces as patterns; label tops of lining pieces. Stitch swag pieces together in ½" (1.3 cm) seams, easing to fit; repeat for the lining pieces. Press the seams open.

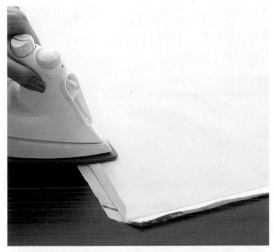

6 Pin the lining to swag, right sides together. Stitch a ½" (1.3 cm) seam around all sides, leaving an opening along upper edge for turning. Trim corners diagonally. Press lining seam allowance toward the lining.

7 Turn the swag right side out; press seamed edges. Slipstitch opening closed. Fanfold swag along seamlines; tie folds with twill tape. Hang swag through scarf ring or over medallion-style scarf holder or tieback holder. Arrange folds in swag and sides as desired. Remove twill tape.

HOW TO MEASURE FOR A SCARF SWAG WITH MULTIPLE SWOOPS

 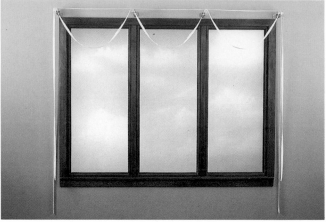

1 Mount swag holders in desired locations. Drape a length of twill tape over the holders as shown, extending to longest points of tapered sides, stretching straight across top of window. This will be the finished length on the top of the swag.

2 Drape a second length of twill tape over the holders, as shown, extending to shortest points of tapered sides, dipping to lowest point desired at center of each swoop. This will be the finished length on the bottom of the swag. Mark both tapes at holders.

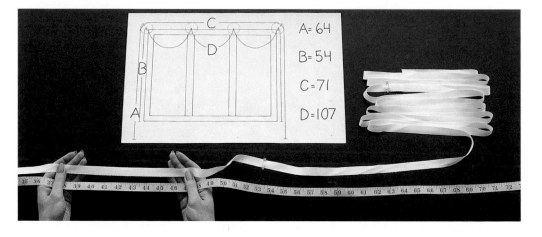

3 Measure and record the lengths of the tape for each section. Measurement A is from the long point to the holder, Measurement B is from the short point to the holder, Measurement C is the distance straight across between the holders, and Measurement D is the total length of all the swoops between end holders.

HOW TO MAKE A SCARF SWAG WITH MULTIPLE SWOOPS

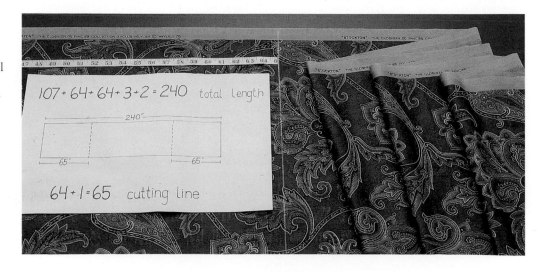

1 Cut the full width of fabric, with length equal to Measurement D plus two times Measurement A plus 1" (2.5 cm) for each swoop plus an additional 2" (5 cm). Measure from each end of the fabric a distance equal to Measurement A plus 1" (2.5 cm). Cut the fabric perpendicular to the selvage at these points. Follow steps 2 and 3 on pages 80 and 81 for swag with single swoop.

2 Measure the length of the center section; divide this measurement into number of swoops in the swag. Mark the center section into lengths of this size; cut the fabric perpendicular to selvages at these points.

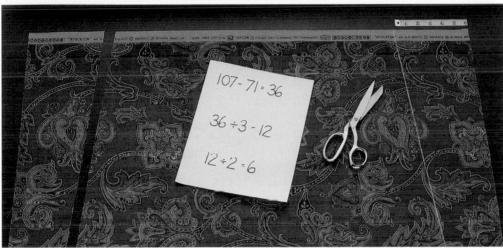

107 - 71 = 36

36 ÷ 3 - 12

12 ÷ 2 = 6

3 Subtract Measurement C from Measurement D. Divide this measurement by the number of swoops in the swag; then divide this number in half. Mark a point on upper edge of one swoop piece this distance from outer edge. Draw a line from this point to lower corner; cut away triangular wedge. Repeat for opposite side of swoop piece. Cut identical wedges from each remaining swoop piece. Complete swag as on page 81, steps 5 to 8.

HOW TO MAKE A SCARF SWAG WITH POUFS

Measurement A 93"
Pout 20'
Seam Allowance 1"
114"

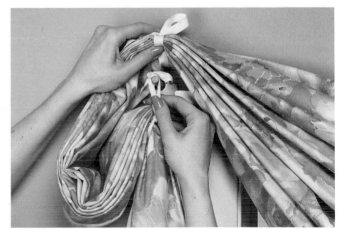

1 Cut the fabric, following step 1 on page 80 for swag with single swoop or step 1, opposite, for swag with multiple swoops, adding 16" to 20" (40.5 to 51 cm) for each pouf. Measure from each end of fabric a distance equal to Measurement A plus length allowed for one pouf plus 1" (2.5 cm). Cut fabric perpendicular to the selvage at these points. Turn one end panel around as on page 80, step 2 (bottom), if using fabric with one-way design.

2 Trim wedges from the end pieces, as on page 81, step 3. Then follow steps 4 to 8 on page 81 for a swag with a single swoop or steps 2 and 3, above, for a swag with multiple swoops; keep folds tied. Tie another piece of twill tape around the fanfolded fabric 16" to 20" (40.5 to 51 cm) below swag holder. Raise tied fabric to the swag holder bracket; knot securely. Fan out fabric to form pouf. Remove upper twill tape.

STAGECOACH VALANCES

Stagecoaches of the Old West were often fitted with simple shades that were rolled up from the bottom and tied in place. A variation of this shade makes a unique stationary valance.

The lower edge of the valance is rolled around a length of PVC plastic pipe, exposing the matching or contrasting lining, and tied with straps of fabric to give the illusion of an operating shade. If a patterned lining is used or if the lining is darker than the valance fabric, interline the treatment to prevent the lining from showing through to the front of the valance when light shines through the window.

The stagecoach valance is attached to a mounting board and can be installed inside or outside the window frame. When installed inside the frame, the ends of the PVC pipe are covered with matching fabric. For an outside mount, returns are added to the sides of the valance above the roll, and finials can be attached to the ends of the pipe.

Space the straps 24" to 36" (61 to 91.5 cm) apart, with the outer straps equal distances from the sides of the valance. For a valance that is wider than the fabric width, railroad the fabric (page 21) to eliminate the need for seams. If railroading is not possible, try to plan the placement of the seams to fall under the straps.

MATERIALS

- Decorator fabric, for valance and covered mounting board.
- Matching or contrasting fabric, for lining.
- Contrasting fabric, for straps.
- Drapery lining, for interlining, if necessary.
- 1¼" (3.2 cm) PVC pipe, cut to finished width of valance.
- Finials designed to fit 1⅜" (3.5 cm) wood pole and industrial-strength adhesive, for outside-mounted valance, optional.
- 1 × 2 mounting board for inside mount, length as determined on page 16.

- Mounting board for outside mount, length and width determined as on page 16.
- Angle irons with flat-head screws, for installing an outside-mounted valance, with length of angle irons more than one-half the projection of the board.
- 8 × 2½" (6.5 cm) flat-head screws, for installing an outside-mounted valance into wall studs; or molly bolts or toggle anchors, for installing outside-mounted valance into drywall or plaster.
- 8 × 1½" (3.8 cm) round-head screws, for installing an inside-mounted valance.
- Masking tape; staple gun and staples.
- Drill and ⅛" drill bit.

Stagecoach valance (above) is mounted outside the window frame. Decorative finials are attached to the ends of the PVC pipe that supports the fabric roll at the lower edge of the valance.

Inside-mounted stagecoach valance (right) is mounted flush with the front of the window frame and the ends of the pipe are capped with fabric.

Determine the finished length and width of the valance. For an inside-mounted valance, the width is ¼" (6 mm) less than the inside measurement of the window frame. For an outside-mounted valance, the finished width must be at least 1½" (3.8 cm) wider than the outside measurement of the frame, to allow the necessary space to mount the angle irons at the sides of the frame.

Cut the fabric for the valance with the length equal to the desired finished length of the valance plus 1½" (3.8 cm) for mounting plus 12" (30.5 cm) to roll onto the PVC pipe at the lower edge plus ½" (1.3 cm) seam allowance. For an inside-mounted valance, the cut width of the fabric is equal to the finished width of the valance plus 1" (2.5 cm) for seam allowances. For an

outside-mounted valance, the cut width of the fabric is equal to the finished width of the valance plus twice the projection of the mounting board plus ½" (1.3 cm) for seam allowances.

Cut the lining fabric to the same length and width as the valance fabric. Also cut the interlining, if desired, to the same length and width as the valance fabric.

For each strap, cut two fabric strips the entire width of the fabric, with the width of each strip equal to twice the desired finished width of the strap plus ½" (1.3 cm) for seam allowances.

Cut the fabric to cover the mounting board (page 16).

HOW TO SEW AN INSIDE-MOUNTED STAGECOACH VALANCE

1 Seam fabric widths together, if necessary. Pin the interlining, if desired, to wrong side of the valance fabric; stitch to the valance fabric ⅜" (1 cm) from all edges. Pin valance fabric and lining fabric right sides together, matching the raw edges.

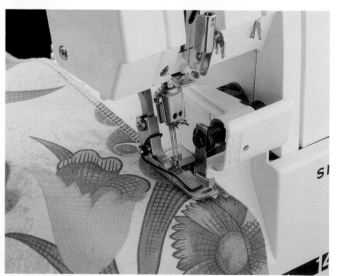

2 Stitch ½" (1.3 cm) seam around sides and lower edge. Trim seam allowances at lower corners diagonally. Press the lining seam allowance toward lining.

3 Turn valance right side out; press seamed edges. Finish upper edge of valance, using overlock or zigzag stitch.

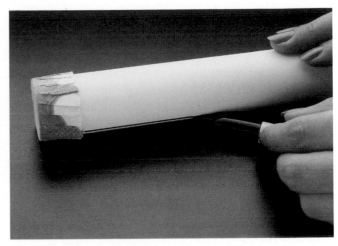

4 Cut two 3" (7.5 cm) circles of decorator fabric. On wrong side, trace circumference of pipe at center of each circle. Clip at ½" (1.3 cm) intervals from the outer edge to the inner marked circle. Glue to ends of PVC pipe, using craft glue.

5 Hold the pipe firmly in place on a table; place a marker flat on the table and slide it down the length of the pipe, to mark line down center of pipe.

6 Center the pipe on right side of valance at lower edge; tape in place, aligning the lower edge of valance to the marked line on pipe, using masking tape.

7 Roll up the valance to desired finished length. Anchor pipe in place with pins.

8 Fold fabric strips for straps in half lengthwise, right sides together. Stitch long edge and one short end, using ¼" (6 mm) seam allowance. Trim across corners diagonally, turn strap right side out, and press. Two straps are used at each placement.

9 Mark desired placement of straps at upper edge of the valance. Cover the mounting board (page 16); staple valance to the board, lapping upper edge of valance 1½" (3.8 cm) onto the top of board. Do not place staples at markings for straps.

(Continued)

HOW TO SEW AN INSIDE-MOUNTED STAGECOACH VALANCE
(CONTINUED)

10 Sandwich valance between two straps at placement marks; tack in place, using pushpins. Tie finished ends; adjust length of straps from upper edge, for desired effect, making sure all straps are the same length. Staple straps to board. Trim excess straps at top.

11 Mount the valance (page 17). Hand-tack rolled fabric to the front straps, catching only the back layer of fabric on straps. Remove pins that anchor valance to pipe.

HOW TO SEW AN OUTSIDE-MOUNTED STAGECOACH VALANCE

1 Seam the fabric widths together, if necessary. Fold the fabric in half lengthwise, right sides together. At raw edge opposite the fold, mark a distance 12½" (31.8 cm) up from lower edge.

2 Draw a line in from the side at mark, parallel to lower edge, with the length equal to the depth of return. Draw a connecting line, parallel to side, down to lower edge; cut out the section through both layers. The width at the lower edge should now be the finished width of valance plus 1" (2.5 cm).

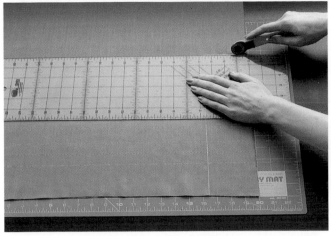

3 Repeat step 2 for lining, and for interlining, if used. Pin the interlining, if used, to wrong side of valance fabric; stitch ⅜" (1 cm) from all sides.

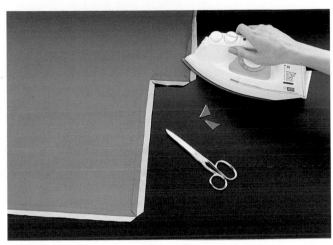

4 Pin valance fabric and lining fabric right sides together, matching raw edges. Stitch ½" (1.3 cm) seam around sides and lower edge. Clip and trim corners. Press lining seam allowances toward lining.

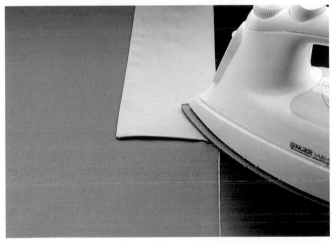

5 Turn valance right side out; press seamed edges. Finish upper edge of valance, using overlock or zigzag stitch. Press returns lightly.

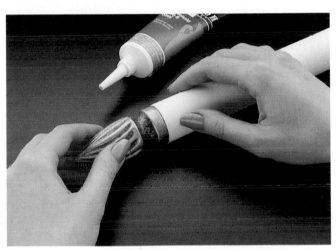

6 Cover ends of the pipe with fabric, if desired, as on page 87, step 4. Or, for pipe with finials, sand ends of pipe smooth; glue finials to ends of pipe, using industrial-strength adhesive. Follow steps 5 to 8 on page 87.

7 Mark desired placement of straps at upper edge of valance. Mark the top of mounting board 1½" (3.8 cm) from front edge. Staple valance to covered mounting board (page 16), aligning the upper edge of valance to marked line and with the returns extending at the ends of the board. Do not place staples at markings for straps.

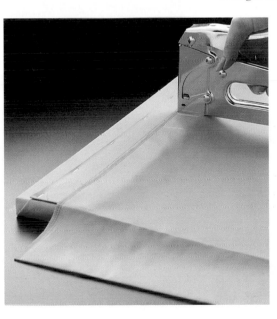

8 Miter corners of returns; staple in place. Finish the valance as in steps 10 and 11, opposite.

BUTTONED VALANCES

Box-pleated valances give window treatments the look of tailored simplicity. With the lower corners of the pleats buttoned back, the contrasting fabric of the pleat inserts is revealed.

These valances are self-lined, eliminating the need for a lower hem. If the valance or the insert fabric is patterned and either lightweight or light in color, the valance should be interlined with lining fabric. Otherwise, the pattern of the self-lining would show through to the right side of the valance, especially with sunlight shining on the treatment.

Pleats are positioned at the outer front corners of the valance. If the projection of the mounting board is less than 5" (12.5 cm), the pleats are not buttoned back on the return sides of the corners. The number of remaining pleats and the spaces between them varies, depending on the size of the window, the desired valance length, and other design considerations. In some cases, it may be desirable to align pleats with existing divisions in the window space created by moldings or mullions, as shown in the diagram at right.

When planning the number of pleats and the spacing, also consider the fabric you are using. You may want to repeat a large motif in each space between the pleats, or perhaps a series of stripes. In general, a fabric with a solid color or a small all-over print can be divided into smaller spaces than a fabric with a large print. The wider the spaces and the larger the print, the more massive the valance will appear.

CALCULATING THE SPACES & PLEATS

Determine the finished width, length, and projection of the valance (page 18). It is helpful to diagram the window treatment. The spaces between the pleats should be at least 10" (25.5 cm) to allow enough room for them to button back. For a valance with evenly spaced pleats, determine the width of the spaces. To do this, first divide the approximate desired space measurement into the width of the valance, rounding up or down to the nearest whole number; this is the number of spaces between the pleats. Divide this number into the valance width to determine the exact measurement of each space. Including the pleats at the outer front corners, there will be one more pleat in the valance than the number of spaces.

MAKING A DIAGRAM

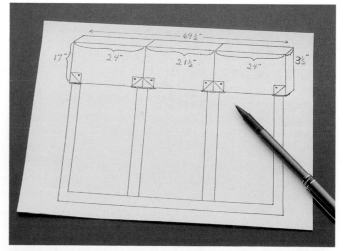

Diagram the window treatment, including any undertreatments. Label the finished length and width of the valance. Plan the placement of the buttoned pleats, with a pleat at each corner. Label the exact width of each space. Label the depth of the return.

MATERIALS

- Decorator fabric, for main valance fabric.

- Contrasting decorator fabric, for the pleat inserts.

- Lining fabric, for the interlining, if a lightweight or light-colored patterned fabric is used for valance or inserts.

- Covered buttons or decorative buttons in the desired size; one button is needed for each corner that will be folded back.

- Mounting board, cut to length as determined on page 16.

- Angle irons with flat-head screws; length of angle iron should be more than one-half the projection of board.

- 8 × 2½" (6.5 cm) flat-head screws for installing valance into wall studs; or molly bolts or toggle anchors for installing into drywall or plaster.

- Staple gun and staples.

Buttoned valances *have many design options. The look can be varied, as shown in the examples above, by changing the spacing between the pleats and the way the pleats are folded back.*

From the main valance fabric, cut the fabric for each space section with the cut width equal to the finished width of the space plus 1" (2.5 cm) for seam allowances; the cut length is equal to twice the finished length of the valance plus 3" (7.5 cm) for mounting.

From the main valance fabric, cut the fabric for each return section with the cut width equal to the projection of the mounting board plus 1" (2.5 cm); the cut length is equal to twice the finished length of the valance plus 3" (7.5 cm).

If the projection of the mounting board is more than 5" (12.5 cm), cut the contrasting fabric for all the pleat inserts 21" (53.5 cm) wide, with the cut length of the inserts equal to twice the finished length of the valance plus 3" (7.5 cm).

If the projection of the mounting board is less than 5" (12.5 cm), cut the contrasting fabric for the two corner pleat inserts with the cut width of each insert equal to twice the projection of the mounting board plus 11" (28 cm). For each remaining pleat insert, cut the contrasting fabric 21" (53.5 cm) wide. The cut length of all the pleat inserts is equal to twice the finished length of the valance plus 3" (7.5 cm).

If interlining is desired, the cut width of the lining fabric is equal to the total width of the valance after the valance seams are stitched. The cut length of the lining fabric is equal to the finished length of the valance plus 1½" (3.8 cm).

Cut the fabric to cover the mounting board (page 16).

HOW TO SEW A VALANCE WITH BUTTONED PLEATS

1 Pin the pleat insert for left end of the valance over the left return section, right sides together; stitch ½" (1.3 cm) seam.

2 Pin a space section to the pleat insert, right sides together; stitch ½" (1.3 cm) seam. Continue to join sections, alternating pleat inserts and space sections; end with the right pleat insert and the right return section. Press seams open.

3 Fold the end of the valance in half lengthwise, right sides together. Sew ½" (1.3 cm) seam on outer edge of returns; turn valance right side out, and press. Repeat for the opposite end of valance.

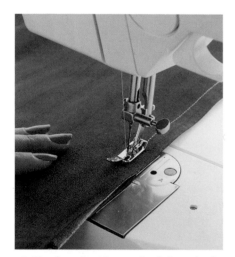

4 Press valance in half, matching raw edges and seams. Machine-baste layers together, ½" (1.3 cm) from raw edges at top of valance.

5 Mark center of each pleat insert along upper and lower edges. If return is less than 5" (12.5 cm), measure from inner seam of return a distance equal to twice the return; pin-mark.

6 Fold under pleats at all seamlines; press. Bring the pressed seams together to pin marks; pin pleats in place along upper and lower edges.

7 Press folded edges of all pleats, turning valance back and pressing only on the pleat, to avoid imprinting edges to right side of valance.

8 Stitch pleats in place across the valance, 1½" (3.8 cm) from upper edge. Finish the upper edge, using overlock or zigzag stitch.

9 Fold back lower corners of pleats at desired angle to expose pleat insert. Pin in place; press, if desired.

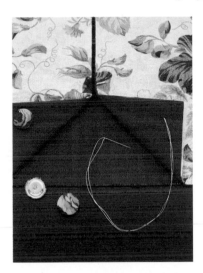

10 Determine button placement. Sew the buttons in place through all layers. For shank style buttons, cut a small slit in the fabric, through corner layers only. Insert the shank through the slit; sew button through remaining layers.

11 Cover mounting board (page 16). Position the valance on the mounting board, using stitching line as guide to extend upper edge 1½" (3.8 cm) onto top of board; position end pleats at the front corners of board. Clip fabric at corner pleats close to stitching line. Staple the valance in place, beginning with returns; ease or stretch valance slightly to fit board, if necessary. Mount the valance (page 17).

HOW TO SEW AN INTERLINED VALANCE WITH BUTTONED PLEATS

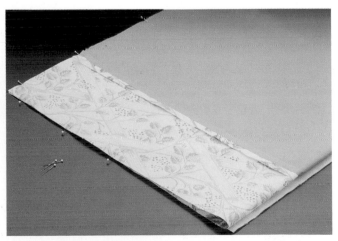

1 Follow steps 1 and 2, opposite; measure the width of seamed valance. For interlining, cut the lining fabric to this measurement, seaming widths together as necessary. Pin interlining to wrong side of valance, matching upper edges and ends.

2 Complete valance as in steps 3 to 11, opposite. The lower edge of interlining extends to the lower fold of valance.

Soft cornices *may consist of a single padded panel (above) or, for more depth, of overlapping panels (right). Welting trims the lower edges and returns, but is optional at the top of the cornice.*

SOFT CORNICES

The soft cornice is a versatile top treatment with limitless possibilities. Lighter in weight and easier to construct than a traditional upholstered cornice, this softer version can be designed to work well in any decorating scheme.

A soft cornice can be constructed as a single panel of fabric with a shaped lower edge. Or, to add depth and texture to the treatment, it can be created with overlapping panels. Whichever style you select, use these basic construction steps as a springboard to creating truly unique soft cornices for your home.

Welting defines the lower and return edges of the soft cornice. For added definition, welting may also trim the upper edge; or, for a softer look, the welting may be omitted along the upper edge.

Decorator fabric is backed with fleece for a padded effect. To prevent the shadowing of any seams or overlapped panels, the cornice is lined with blackout lining.

The mounting board for the soft cornice is constructed with legs at the return ends to give the treatment added support. The finished width of the soft cornice must be at least 3" (7.5 cm) wider than the outside measurement of the window frame; this allows the necessary space at the side of the window frame for the legs and angle irons. Follow the basic guidelines on page 16 to determine the projection of the soft cornice and to mount the finished project.

As with any window treatment, it is important to diagram the soft cornice to scale. Hang a full-size paper pattern over the window before beginning the actual project, to check the measurements and proportion.

MATERIALS

- Decorator fabric for the soft cornice, hem facing, covered mounting board and legs, and dustcover.
- Contrasting decorator fabric and ½" (1.3 cm) cording, for welting.
- Flexible curve or curved ruler.
- Paper-backed fusible web.
- Polyester fleece.
- Blackout lining.
- Glue stick; heavy-duty stapler and staples.
- Mounting board and side legs; 8 × 2½" (6.5 cm) flat-head

screws, for connecting legs to mounting board.
- Cardboard stripping.
- Self-adhesive hook and loop tape.
- Angle irons with flat-head screws; length of angle irons should be more than one-half the width of the mounting board.
- 8 × 2½" (6.5 cm) flat head screws for installing soft cornice directly into wall studs; or molly bolts or toggle anchors for installing soft cornice into drywall or plaster.

DIAGRAMING THE SOFT CORNICE

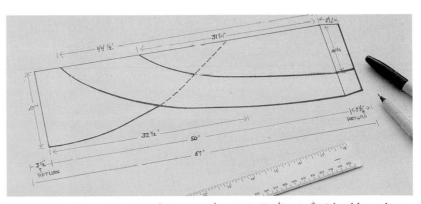

Diagram soft cornice to scale on graph paper. Indicate finished length at longest and shortest points, projection of mounting board, and finished width of cornice including returns. Indicate placement of welting with heavy lines; include ½" (1.3 cm) welting at lower edge and returns in finished length and width measurements. For cornice with overlapping panels, draw the shape of overlapped panels with dotted lines, and indicate the measurements of each panel.

For a single-panel soft cornice, cut the fabric with the length equal to the finished length at the longest point plus a 2" (5 cm) margin at top and bottom. The cut width of the fabric is equal to the finished width plus twice the projection of the mounting board plus a 2" (5 cm) margin on each side. If the cut width exceeds the fabric width, railroad the fabric (page 21) whenever possible, to avoid any seams. For fabric that cannot be railroaded, cut one fabric width for the center of the panel, and seam equal partial widths to each side, matching the pattern in the fabric.

For a soft cornice with overlapping panels, make the paper pattern pieces as on page 100, step 1. Cut the fabric, adding a 2" (5 cm) margin around each pattern piece.

Cut the polyester fleece, paper-backed fusible web, and blackout lining to the same size as the decorator fabric; the fusible web may be cut in several pieces, if necessary, butting the pieces together as they are applied.

For a single-panel soft cornice, cut one facing strip from the decorator fabric to the same width as the lining. To determine the cut length of the strip, subtract the shortest point of the cornice from the longest point; then add 3½" (9 cm). For a cornice with overlapping panels, cut facing strips for the panels on the return ends only. From the contrasting fabric, cut bias strips, 2½" (6.5 cm) wide, to cover the cording for the welting.

Cut the mounting board (page 16). Cut two side legs with the same projection as the mounting board, each 3" (7.5 cm) shorter than the finished length of the soft cornice at the return. Cut the fabric for the dustcover 1" (2.5 cm) wider and longer than the width and length of the mounting board.

HOW TO MAKE A SINGLE-PANEL SOFT CORNICE

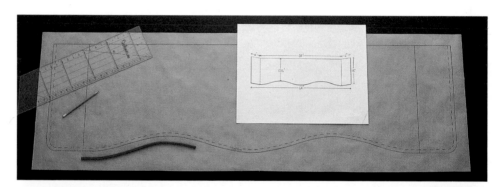

1 Draw full-size pattern of soft cornice, including returns, following scaled diagram (page 95); the ½" (1.3 cm) welting at lower edge and returns is included in the finished size. Use designing tool, such as flexible curve or curved ruler, to draw curved lines along lower edge of pattern. Round corners.

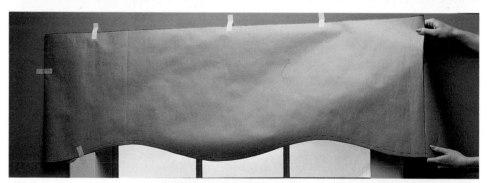

2 Cut out pattern; do not add seam allowances, because the ½" (1.3 cm) allowance for the welting compensates for seam allowances. Hang pattern in the desired location at top of the window; check for accurate measurements and proportion.

3 Place fabric facedown on pressing surface. Apply paper-backed fusible web to wrong side of fabric, following manufacturer's instructions; butt pieces of fusible web together as necessary.

4 Remove the paper backing from fusible web. Place the polyester fleece over fusible web; fuse in place, pressing from fleece side. Turn over; press again from right side of fabric.

5 Place the pattern on right side of padded fabric, positioning pattern as desired for design of fabric; pin in place within seam allowances. Cut out soft cornice along sides and lower edge; do not trim off the excess fabric at the top.

6 Press under ½" (1.3 cm) seam allowance along upper edge of facing strip. Lay facing strip over lining, right sides up, matching lower and side edges; glue-baste upper seam allowance of facing strip to lining.

7 Turn up the facing strip; stitch along pressed line. Turn the facing strip back down, realigning lower edges.

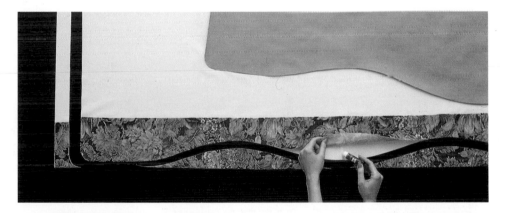

8 Place pattern facedown over the right side of lining piece, with the longest points of lower edge even with lower edge of the facing strip; pin within seam allowances. Cut out lining along the sides and lower edge; do not trim off excess fabric at the top. Glue-baste lower edge of facing strip to lining.

9 Make covered welting as on page 48, steps 1 to 3. Machine-baste welting to right side of padded fabric along sides and lower edge, matching raw edges and stitching a scant ½" (1.3 cm) from the edges. Clip and ease welting at corners and curves.

10 Pin welted fabric to lining within seam allowances, right sides together. Stitch ½" (1.3 cm) seam along the sides and lower edge, crowding the welting. Clip seam allowances on curves; trim corners. Turn soft cornice right side out; press.

(Continued)

11 Measure desired finished length from lower edge of the cornice; mark a line on the lining side. Mark a second line 1½" (3.8 cm) above the first line.

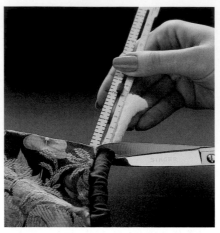

12 Cut along second line through all layers. Pull out cords at the ends of the welting; cut off 2" (5 cm) of cording.

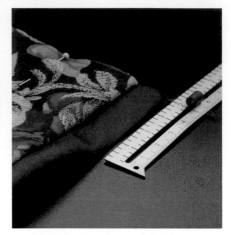

13 Pull seam to return the cords to original position. Finish upper edge by stitching through all layers, using zigzag or overlock stitch.

14 Cover mounting board and legs separately as on page 16, except attach fabric so fold is along the long edge of board as shown. Stand mounting board and leg on edge, with stapled sides facing outward; butt top of leg to underside of mounting board, with the outside edges even.

15 Predrill holes for two screws through mounting board into end of leg; insert screws. Repeat for other leg.

16 Support leg over edge of table; staple the hook side of hook and loop tape ½" (1.3 cm) from the back outer edge of leg, from the top of mounting board to the bottom of the leg. Repeat for opposite leg.

17 Cut two strips of loop tape to the same lengths as hook tape applied to legs. Affix to the lining at return edges of soft cornice, just inside the welting, with top of the tape at the marked line.

18 Place mounting board on lining side of the soft cornice, with front edge of the board facedown and the upper edge of the top board even with the marked line. Secure returns to legs with hook and loop tape.

19 Support mounting board on edge of work surface; staple the upper edge of soft cornice to the top of mounting board, clipping and overlapping fabric at corners. For soft cornice without welting at the upper edge, omit steps 20 and 21.

20 Trim ½" (1.3 cm) of cording out of end of welting; tuck fabric into end, encasing cord. Staple welting to top of mounting board, along the outer edge, beginning at back of board; allow welting to overhang cornice slightly. Staple to within 3" (7.5 cm) of opposite end.

21 Cut welting ½" (1.3 cm) beyond back edge of board. Trim ½" (1.3 cm) of cording out of end of welting; tuck fabric into end, encasing cord. Finish stapling welting to board.

22 Place dustcover facedown on cornice, with 1" (2.5 cm) extending over front edge onto top of mounting board and equal amounts extending at sides. Place cardboard stripping over dustcover, with edge of stripping along front edge of mounting board; if welting has been applied to upper edge, lay stripping even with seam of welt. Staple in place.

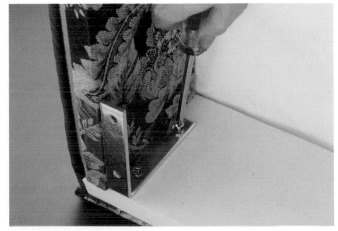

23 Fold back dustcover over cardboard stripping; fold under excess fabric on ends and along the back of the mounting board. Staple in place.

24 Mount soft cornice as on page 17, placing outer angle irons just inside legs of mounting board.

HOW TO MAKE A SOFT CORNICE WITH OVERLAPPING PANELS

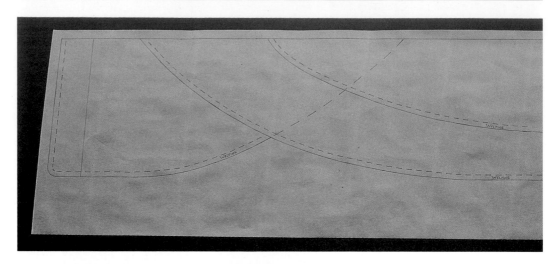

1 Draw a full-size pattern of the soft cornice, including the returns, following the scaled diagram (page 95). Draw separate patterns for each overlapping panel; include ½" (1.3 cm) welting in the finished size of each panel.

2 Tape pattern together as it is to be constructed, using removable tape. Hang in desired location at top of the window; check for accurate measurements and proportion.

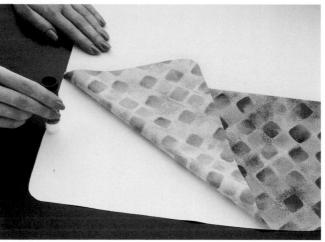

3 Separate the pattern pieces. For each panel of soft cornice, follow steps 3 to 5 on pages 96 and 97; for panels on return ends, apply facing strips as in steps 6 and 7. Continue as in steps 8 to 17 for all panels.

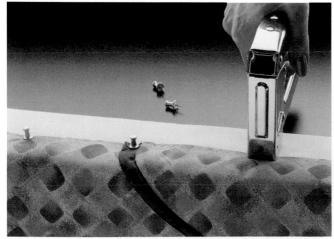

4 Arrange the panels on the mounting board in desired placement, tacking them in place temporarily, using pushpins. Secure return sides to legs of mounting board with hook and loop tape. Staple panels to mounting board.

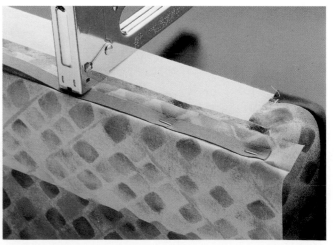

5 Follow steps 20 and 21 on page 99 if welting is desired along the upper edge. For a cornice with or without welting, complete the cornice as in steps 22 to 24.

MORE IDEAS
FOR SOFT
CORNICES

Triangle-point soft cornice
(right) has overlapping panels
and is trimmed with welting. For
easier application of the welting,
the points are slightly rounded.

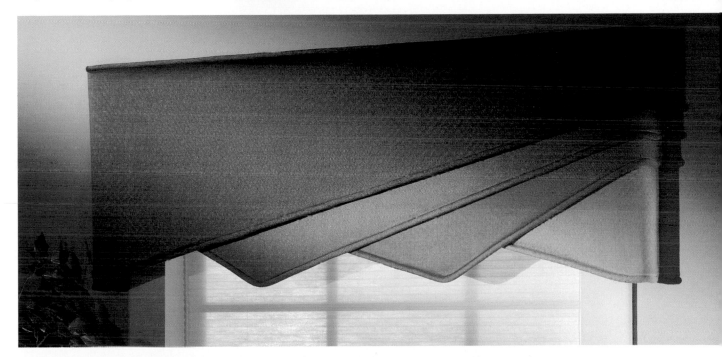

Soft cornice
with overlapping
panels *(above)*
is made using a
different fabric for
each panel.

Single-panel soft
cornice *(left) is*
shaped at the lower
edge to follow the
motifs in the fabric.

Alternatives
&
Embellishments

HANGING PLANT SHELVES

Plants have a delightful way of adding charm and hospitality to a room, no matter what the decorating scheme may be. Placed on a hanging plant shelf, the plants receive the necessary light and serve as an attractive window treatment. Located near the top of the window, a single hanging shelf with several hanging or climbing plants becomes a valance. A double or triple hanging shelf, hung to cover the entire window or just the lower half, acts as a curtain when filled with plants.

The shelves, made from 1 × 6 stock lumber, are braced with parting stop at each end and suspended with rope from a wooden pole. When the pole is mounted at the top of a wide window, an additional brace and rope can be added to the center, along with a center support bracket for the pole.

The ropes are knotted just below the pole and under each brace to keep the shelf hanging level. If desired, holes can be cut into the shelf to hold pots that have slanted sides and collars, such as standard clay pots. Vary the number of the shelves and the space between them, depending on the size of the window, the height of the plants, and the desired placement of the plant shelves.

SELECTING PLANTS

Select plants for the hanging shelf according to the light requirements of the plants. Also consider other habits and features of the plants, such as the plant colors, their direction of growth, the size they will become, and their tolerance. Place plants of different sizes, shapes, and colors next to each other for contrast, or place several similar plants together for a more uniform look.

Holes cut into this hanging plant shelf hold potted plants of various colors, sizes, and shapes.

MATERIALS

- 1 × 6 boards, preferably of grade #2 or better.
- Parting stop.
- 180-grit or 220-grit sandpaper.
- Drill and 5/16" drill bit; 3/32" combination drill and countersink bit.
- 6 × 1" (2.5 cm) flat-head sheet-metal screws.
- 3/16" (4.5 mm) nylon or polyester rope.
- Wood pole, 1 3/8" (3.5 cm) in diameter, and finials.
- Pole brackets with 4" to 6" (10 to 15 cm) projection; center support bracket for pole measuring 36" (91.5 cm) or more, mounted at the top of a window.
- Latex paint, or wood stain and clear acrylic finish; sponge applicator.

CUTTING DIRECTIONS

Cut a 1 × 6 board for each shelf, with the length of the board equal to the outside measurement of the window frame. For the end braces under each shelf, cut two 7" (18 cm) lengths of parting stop. If the shelves are more than 36" (91.5 cm) wide, cut a third brace for the center of each shelf.

The brackets for the wood pole are mounted as on page 107, step 10. Then, cut the wood pole 2" (5 cm) longer than the distance from the outer edge of one bracket to the outer edge of the other bracket. Cut a piece of rope for each end and for the center, if needed, with the length equal to twice the distance from the top of the pole to the bottom of the lowest shelf plus 6" (15 cm) for the upper knot plus 6" (15 cm) for each knot under each shelf plus an extra 6" to 10" (15 to 25.5 cm). Wrap tape around the cords before cutting, to prevent raveling.

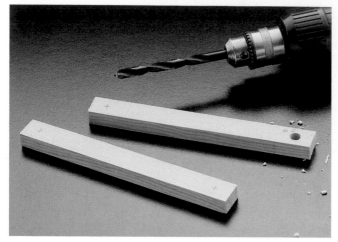

1 Mark placement of holes for rope on the wide side of braces, ½" (1.3 cm) from each end; drill holes, using 5⁄16" drill bit.

2 Sand all wood surfaces, using 180-grit or 220-grit sandpaper; round the corners of the shelves and braces slightly.

3 Mark lines on underside of shelf 2" (5 cm) from each end. On wide side of braces, mark placement for screws, 1½" (3.8 cm) from ends. Place braces, wide side up, on shelf, with outer edges along lines and ends extending equally on each side of shelf. Position a third brace, if needed, at center of board. Repeat for braces on any additional shelves.

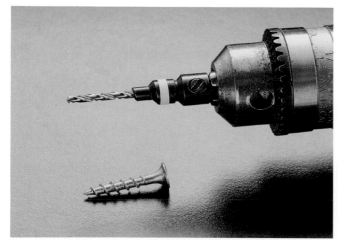

4 Adjust 3⁄32" combination drill and countersink bit as shown, so head of the drywall screw will be recessed below surface of wood when inserted into drilled hole; tighten set screw.

5 Predrill screw holes, holding the brace firmly in place as positioned in step 3; drill through brace and into underside of shelf, up to point on drill bit indicated by white line. Insert 6 × 1" (2.5 cm) drywall screw. Repeat for remaining braces.

6 Paint the shelves, if desired, or stain shelves and apply clear acrylic finish.

7 Fold the ropes in half. Tie each folded rope together in an overhand knot near the folded end, leaving a 2½" (6.5 cm) loop; tie all knots in the same direction so they look the same. Place ropes on work surface, aligning the ends and knots.

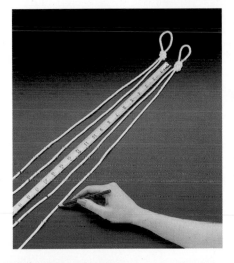

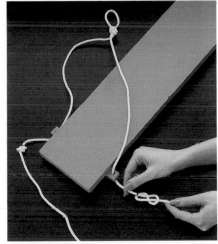

8 Measure from the overhand knots to the desired location for the first set of shelf support knots, allowing 1¼" (3.2 cm) for the thickness of the shelf and braces. Mark the ropes with pencil.

9 Thread the rope down through the holes in the braces of the shelf until the pencil marks are below the braces. As shown, tie a figure-eight knot at each location, just under mark.

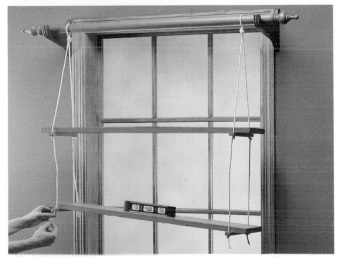

10 Repeat steps 8 and 9 for any additional shelves, measuring from previous knots. Mount brackets for wood pole, either on the window frame or just outside the frame; use molly bolts or toggle anchors if not installing the brackets into window frame or wall studs. If a center support bracket is needed, mount it with one side of bracket at center.

11 Slide the pole through loops in the rope, and attach finials to ends; mount the pole on brackets. Check to see that shelves are level and resting on knots; adjust the knots if necessary. Trim excess rope under the knots for the bottom shelf.

1 Mark placement for the ropes and drill holes as on page 106, step 1. Measure the circumference of flowerpot just under collar. Divide this measurement by 6.28 to determine radius. Draw a circle with this radius on paper, using a compass.

2 Cut out the circle; slide it over the bottom of the pot up to the collar; adjust the size of the hole, if necessary.

3 Determine the number of holes and spacing between them; the outer edge of first and last holes should be at least 3½" (9 cm) from the end of the shelf, and the minimum spacing between holes is 2" (5 cm). Mark circles for the holes on top of the shelf.

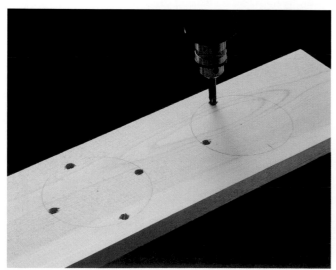

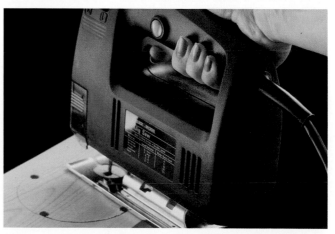

4 Drill four evenly spaced holes at inner edge of each circle, using large drill bit.

5 Insert jigsaw blade into drilled hole; cut on marked line up to next hole. Turn board, and continue sawing, turning board at each hole until entire circle is cut out. Repeat for remaining holes. Complete plant shelf as on pages 106 and 107, steps 2 to 11.

Potted ivy plants, *hung at the sides of a window, climb the honeysuckle vine over the window frame. Secure the honeysuckle vines by wrapping them with wire and twisting the wire around screw eyes inserted into the window frame or wall. Loosely tie ivy stems to the honeysuckle vine, using string or plant ties; train new growth to climb by gently weaving it through the vine.*

Spider plants *(above), suspended from the ceiling at different heights, create an arched valance. The plant hangers with clear monofilament line are hung from ceiling hooks.*

African violets *(right) are hung at the sides of tieback curtains, using wall brackets designed for holding pots. Make the curtains as on pages 44 to 47, and make the shaped tiebacks as on pages 54 to 57.*

FROSTED WINDOW DESIGNS

Here is a unique window treatment that is applied directly to the windowpane. Frosted glass spray paint provides a durable finish that cuts the glare of strong sunlight and provides privacy for windows in bathrooms or entrances. For a decorative effect, the paint is sprayed over a masking stencil of self-adhesive vinyl. The pieces of the stencil are then removed, revealing a clear design in the frosted glass. By reversing the stenciling process and masking the areas around the design, rather than the design itself, the spray paint can be used to resemble an etched design in the glass. Unlike true etched glass, frosted glass spray paint can be removed, if desired, using a razor blade or lacquer thinner. To clean the frosted glass without removing it, use a mild glass cleaner and wipe gently with a soft cloth.

MATERIALS

- Frosted glass spray paint.
- Self-adhesive vinyl, such as Con-Tact®.
- Mat knife.
- Graphite paper to transfer design, or precut stencil.
- Masking tape; paper.
- Glass cleaner; clean, soft, lint-free cloth.

Frosted glass with clear design (above) provides privacy, making it suitable for entrance windows.

Frosted design (left) adds detailing to a window, while allowing you to enjoy the scenery outside.

HOW TO APPLY A FROSTED GLASS FINISH
WITH A CLEAR DESIGN

1 Clean the window thoroughly, using glass cleaner and a soft, lint-free cloth. Cut self-adhesive vinyl 2" (5 cm) larger than design. Remove paper backing; affix vinyl to window in the desired location, pressing out any air bubbles. If more than one width of vinyl is needed, overlap the edges slightly.

2 Position design on window, with carbon or graphite paper under design; tape in place. Trace design onto vinyl **(a).** Or tape precut stencil to vinyl in desired position; trace design areas with pencil **(b).**

3 Cut around the design areas, using a mat knife, applying just enough pressure to cut through the vinyl. Overcut corners or curves into surrounding areas, if necessary, but do not cut into design areas.

4 Remove vinyl surrounding design areas, using tip of mat knife to lift edge of vinyl.

5 Press firmly on all areas of the design; rub away any traces of adhesive left on glass, using glass cleaner and a soft, lint-free cloth.

6 Mask off the woodwork around window and surrounding wall area, using masking tape and paper, to protect from overspray of the paint.

7 Check to be sure the glass surface is free of dust. Follow the manufacturer's instructions for applying paint. Spray paint onto the window in sweeping motion, holding can 10" to 12" (25.5 to 30.5 cm) away from glass, lightly respraying surface several times in one application. Allow to dry for 15 minutes. Repeat two or three times, for good coverage.

8 Remove vinyl in design areas, using tip of mat knife to lift edge of vinyl. Gently rub away any traces of adhesive left on the glass, using a soft cloth dipped in glass cleaner.

HOW TO APPLY A FROSTED DESIGN
WITH SURROUNDING CLEAR GLASS

1 Follow steps 1 and 2, opposite. Cut around the design areas to be frosted, using a mat knife, applying just enough pressure to cut through the vinyl. At the corners, do not cut past point of the intersecting lines, onto the area surrounding design.

2 Remove vinyl in design areas to be frosted, using tip of mat knife to lift edge of vinyl.

3 Follow step 5, opposite. Mask off woodwork, walls, or any areas of the glass not protected by the stencil, using masking tape and paper.

4 Follow step 7, above, spraying over design area. Remove vinyl, masking tape, and paper. Gently rub away any traces of adhesive left on glass, using a soft, lint-free cloth dipped in glass cleaner.

SHOJI-STYLE
SCREENS

Traditional Japanese screens, called *shoji*, made by highly skilled craftsmen, are an intricate wooden lattice framework backed with rice paper. Muted light filters through the finely textured rice paper, filling the room with an aura of tranquility. A simplified version of the shoji can be easily made using basic tools and skills. These lightweight, stationary panels, with their clean-lined Oriental design, add sophisticated elegance to a room.

The shoji-style screen is made entirely from parting stop, which measures ½" × ¾" (1.3 × 2 cm). Cut from pine and other softwoods, parting stop is inexpensive and readily available at any lumber store. Although the wood in traditional Japanese shoji is left unfinished, this westernized version can be painted or stained, if desired. Traditional Japanese shoji are made with white rice paper, although colored or flecked papers that contain pulp and synthetic fibers can create interesting effects and may be more durable. The paper can be applied in one sheet or in multiple sheets, depending on the size of the paper you are using and the size of the shoji framework.

The screen may be mounted either inside the window frame or on the front of the frame. Careful measuring and cutting is important, especially if the screen will be installed inside the window frame. A frame depth of at least 2" (5 cm) is necessary for an inside mount, to allow the screen to be mounted flush with the front edge of the window frame, yet stand at least 1" (2.5 cm) away from the glass. The screen is made ¼" (6 mm) narrower and shorter than the inside of the window frame and is held in place by self-adhesive bumper pads secured to the outer edges of the screen to create friction between the window frame and the screen.

When the window frame is less than 2" (5 cm) deep, the screen is mounted on the front of the window frame, overlapping the inner edge of the window frame by ½" (1.3 cm). For windows with a sill, the screen overlaps the window frame on the sides and top and rests on the sill. Take accurate measurements of the window and draw a full-size pattern of the screen framework before cutting the wood.

Shoji-style framework *has an inner frame, consisting of two vertical stiles (**a**) and top and bottom rails (**b**), a slightly offset outer frame (**c**), and interior lattice strips (**d**).*

MATERIALS

- Parting stop; an estimate of the length needed can be made after drawing the pattern.
- Rice paper or other sturdy decorative paper.
- Double-stick transfer tape, or adhesive transfer gum (ATG) tape, available at art supply and framing supply stores.
- #6 × 1⅝" (4 cm) zinc-plated drywall screws, or deck screws.
- Wood filler; wood glue; sandpaper.
- Paint, or stain and clear acrylic finish, if desired.
- Self-adhesive bumper pads, ⅛" (3 mm) thick, for mounting the screen inside the window frame.
- Two shoulder hooks and two screw eyes, for mounting the screen on the front of the window frame.
- Mat knife.
- Spring clamps; drill; ⅛" combination drill and countersink bit.
- Small miter box and backsaw.

MAKING THE PATTERN FOR A SHOJI-STYLE SCREEN

1 Measure window frame; determine outer measurements of screen as on page 115. Draw outline of screen on large sheet of paper; use accurate measurements and square corners.

2 Draw the outer frame of screen ½" (1.3 cm) wide; sides run full length of frame, with top and bottom sections abutting sides at inner edges.

3 Draw stiles and rails ½" (1.3 cm) wide, inside outer frame; stiles run the full length between top and bottom sections of outer frame, with rails abutting stiles at inner edges.

4 Draw inner lattice of screen as desired; draw all sections ½" (1.3 cm) wide, abutting the ends of lattice sections to inner edges of stiles, rails, or other lattice sections. Sections should abut each other at right angles. To allow for the insertion of screws, stagger placement of ends that abut opposite sides of the same section. It is helpful to plan the design of the lattice by sketching it on another piece of paper before drawing it on the pattern.

5 Tape the finished pattern to the window frame; check to see that the pattern is accurate.

HOW TO MAKE THE FRAMEWORK FOR A SHOJI-STYLE SCREEN

CUTTING DIRECTIONS

Measure the pattern for the length of each wood section, including the stiles, rails, lattice, and outer frame sections. Keeping the ½" (1.3 cm) side of the parting stop faceup, mark and cut the parting stop for each section, using a pencil; cut on the outside of the line, using a miter box and backsaw, leaving each section slightly longer than the desired finished length.

1 Check the lengths of outer frame sections by placing sections of parting stop over pattern. Sand the ends of sections until they fit the pattern exactly. Reposition on the pattern.

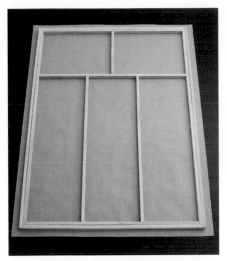

2 Repeat step 1 for stiles, rails, and all lattice sections until the entire framework is laid out on pattern.

3 Remove left stile from pattern, and place it faceup near the edge of a flat work surface. Abut bottom rail to stile, faceup, with lower edges even; clamp. Mark placement for screw on outside of stile, in line with the center of the rail.

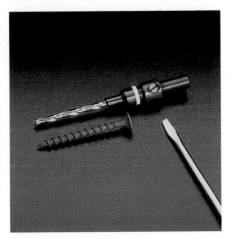

4 Adjust ⅛" combination drill and countersink bit as shown, so head of the drywall screw will be recessed below surface of wood when inserted into drilled hole; tighten set screw.

5 Predrill the screw hole, drilling through side of the stile and into center of the end of rail; countersink the hole up to point on bit indicated by white line. Insert drywall screw.

6 Repeat steps 3 and 5 for top rail. Attach right stile to the opposite end of rails, abutting ends of rails to side of stile; countersink holes, and insert screws.

7 Position the stiles and rails over the lattice pieces on pattern. Align all pieces for perfect fit. Make small pencil lines at every abutting location.

8 Join sections of lattice, working from center outward and aligning penciled markings. Keep lattice flat on work surface, and predrill holes in line with center of section being joined; insert screws.

9 Fit lattice inside the framework of stiles and rails. Join the stiles and rails to lattice, countersinking holes and inserting screws.

10 Apply wood glue to upper side of top rail and top ends of stiles. Place the framework faceup on flat surface; place straightedge of about ⅛" (3 mm) thickness next to top rail. Rest the top section of outer frame on straightedge to offset it slightly; glue to the top rail, aligning ends. Clamp in place.

(Continued)

11 Repeat step 10 for bottom section of outer frame. Then glue side sections of outer frame to stiles, using straightedge to offset them; align ends. Clamp in place until dry.

12 Cover exposed screw heads in lattice with wood filler, if desired. Allow to dry. Repeat if wood filler has shrunk. Sand filled areas until flush with wood surface.

13 Sand any rough areas of the screen lightly. If desired, paint the framework; or stain the framework and apply clear acrylic finish.

HOW TO ATTACH THE PAPER TO A SHOJI-STYLE SCREEN
USING A SINGLE SHEET

1 Cut rice paper 1" (2.5 cm) longer and wider than outer frame. Place screen framework facedown on flat surface; apply double-stick transfer tape to all styles, rails, and lattices.

2 Center piece of paper, right side down, and affix center of each side to frame.

3 Pull paper taut, and affix sides of paper to stiles and rails.

4 Affix the paper to all the lattice sections.

5 Fold back the excess paper at the edges of inner frame; crease. Trim, using mat knife.

HOW TO ATTACH THE PAPER TO A SHOJI-STYLE SCREEN USING MULTIPLE SHEETS

1 Divide original screen pattern into smaller areas if one sheet of paper is not large enough to cover the entire screen. Trace each area onto tracing paper, planning for paper pieces to overlap each other on the back of the lattice sections, hiding seams.

2 Cut each piece of paper, using traced patterns; add a 1" (2.5 cm) margin on each side.

3 Place screen framework facedown on flat surface. Apply double-stick transfer tape to outer edges of first area to be covered and to any lattice strips within the area.

4 Center corresponding piece of paper, right side down, and affix center of each side to frame.

5 Pull paper taut, and affix to edges. Fold back cxccss paper at edges; crease. Trim, using mat knife.

6 Apply paper to adjoining area, overlapping pieces on the back of any adjoining lattice strips. Continue to apply each piece consecutively, working from one end of screen to the other.

HOW TO MOUNT A SHOJI-STYLE SCREEN INSIDE THE WINDOW FRAME

1 Remove the protective cover from self-adhesive bumper pads, and secure to outside edge of outer frame, 2" (5 cm) from each corner. Secure additional pads at 18" to 24" (46 to 61 cm) intervals around outer frame.

2 Push the screen into place inside the window frame until front of screen is flush with front of the window frame. Check for snug fit. Stack additional pads, if necessary.

HOW TO MOUNT A SHOJI-STYLE SCREEN ON THE FRONT OF THE WINDOW FRAME

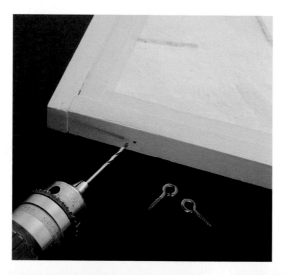

1 Mark placement for screw eyes on top of the outer frame, 2" (5 cm) from the corners. Predrill holes, using a drill bit slightly smaller than diameter of threaded portion of screw eye. Insert screw eyes.

2 Hold screen in place at window, overlapping window frame ½" (1.3 cm). Mark placement for shoulder hooks.

3 Predrill the holes for shoulder hooks, using a drill bit slightly smaller than diameter of threaded portion of hook. Insert hooks.

4 Hang the screen, hooking the screw eyes over the shoulder hooks.

MORE IDEAS FOR DESIGNING SHOJI-STYLE SCREENS

Multicolor screen with a painted frame is mounted over a door window for privacy.

Textured white papers are used for this inside-mounted screen. The screen has been stained to match the window frame.

CREATIVE ALTERNATIVES

Unique window treatments can be created from items intended for other purposes. Consider using beautiful table linens to dress your windows. With a little imagination, a golf club or fishing pole can become a curtain rod, and a favorite collection of hats or fans can be turned into an eye-catching valance. Unexpected elements used as window treatments add charm and personality to your home.

Hanging shelf valance *(page 104) makes an ideal swing for teddy bears in a child's bedroom.*

Embroidered table runners *(above) are draped over swag holders for a simple, yet striking, swag.*

Seining net and creels *(left) balance each other in a rustic display.*

Straw hats (above), adorned with flowers and ribbons, are hung from a peg rail to create a seasonal window valance.

Leather belts buckled over a rolled matchstick blind (right) create a masculine stagecoach valance. When mounting the shade, drill the holes and insert the screws through the belts and the mounting board.

Sports pennants create a fitting treatment for a young sports fan. The pennants are secured to the wood pole with double-stick tape.

FRINGE

The appearance of a window treatment can be changed dramatically, simply by adding fringe. Decorator fringes are available in a wide range of styles and colors, many with coordinating braids, tassels, or tiebacks. They may be made from synthetic or natural fibers or a combination of fibers with interesting textural effects.

Many fringes have decorative headings and should be sewn on the outer surface of the window treatment. Some styles have a plain heading and are intended to be sewn into a seam, encasing the heading and exposing only the fringe.

Consider the length of the fringe when planning the window treatment. Though long fringes offer a dramatic look, they also severely affect the finished length of the treatment.

Brush fringe (1) is a dense row of cotton, or a blend of cotton and synthetic, all cut to the same length. When fringe is purchased, the cut edge is usually secured with a chain stitch, which should be left intact until the application is completed. After removing the chain stitch, fluff out the fringe by steaming and gentle brushing.

Cut fringe (2) has a decorative heading and is similar to brush fringe, but usually not as dense. The cut threads of this fringe are often multicolored in a blend of fibers.

Loop fringe (3) is made with a decorative heading. It is available in cotton, synthetic, or a combination of fibers. Just as the name implies, the fringe is composed of a series of overlapping looped threads. The loops may be all the same length or arranged in a pattern of varying lengths.

Tassel fringe (4) is a continuous row of miniature tassels attached to a decorative heading. The tassels, often separated by loops, may be multicolored or multifibered.

Knot fringe (5) is usually made of long cotton threads that are tied in single or multiple rows of knots just below the plain heading.

Ball fringe (6) is a continuous row of pom-poms hanging from a plain heading. Though recognized as a casual craft fringe, some styles are more ornate and suitable for embellishing window treatments.

Bullion fringe (7) is a continuous row of twisted cords attached to a decorative heading. Styles range from very heavy long fringe to lightweight short fringe with single-color or multicolored cords. Cotton bullion fringe is quite casual, while rayon or acetate bullion fringes can be used for very elegant applications.

TIPS FOR ATTACHING FRINGE

1 **Decorative heading.** Apply liquid fray preventer liberally to area of heading that will be cut; allow to dry completely before cutting fringe.

2 Pin or glue-baste fringe in desired location on right side of finished window treatment, turning under ¾" (2 cm) at ends of heading. Straight-stitch along top and bottom of heading.

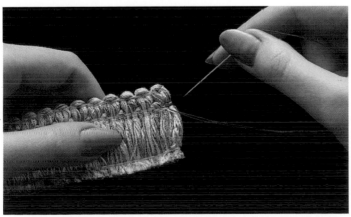

1 **Plain heading.** Cut fringe between loops; hand-stitch cut ends to prevent raveling.

2 Machine-baste fringe to the right side of prepared window treatment panel, placing the fringe heading within the seam allowance. Pin panel and lining right sides together; stitch, encasing fringe heading.

INDEX

Other home decorating books by Creative Publishing international:

*To purchase any of these books, visit your local bookstore
or log on to www.howtobookstore.com*

**CREATIVE
PUBLISHING
international**

AMERICA'S PREMIER HOW-TO PUBLISHER